BRAINWASHING
FOR
BEGINNERS

MEGHAN ROWLAND & CHRIS TURNER-NEAL

Avon, Massachusetts

Published by
Adams Media, a division of F+W Media, Inc.
57 Littlefield Street, Avon, MA 02322. U.S.A.
www.adamsmedia.com

ISBN 10: 1-4405-2861-6
ISBN 13: 978-1-4405-2861-3
eISBN 10: 1-4405-2974-4
eISBN 13: 978-1-4405-2974-0

Printed in the United States of America.

10 9 8 7 6 5 4 3 2 1

Library of Congress Cataloging-in-Publication Data
is available from the publisher.

This book is available at quantity discounts for bulk purchases.
For information, please call 1-800-289-0963.

For Garry Shandling, our rose without a thorn.

Acknowledgments

Parents, friends, family, Matt, and God. You know, the usual.

CONTENTS

INTRODUCTION

HOW TO CHEAT FRIENDS AND INFLUENCE PEOPLE

Kim Jong-Il, despite his prescription aviators and obvious hormone imbalance, rules an entire country. Jerry Falwell, noted loon, had his own *accredited* university that still thrives today. Nick Nolte, Father Time's redheaded stepchild, was *People* magazine's "Sexiest Man Alive" in 1992, well after his youthful good looks were replaced by a tense, haunted expression. Even taking into account alternative explanations like "Them's the breaks" and voodoo, some events are only explicable if everyone involved wasn't thinking clearly. Sure, we could blame food additives or "Scorpio rising," but isn't it simpler or ultimately funnier to think that everyone's been brainwashed? Brainwashing isn't just a war crime—it's a life management strategy. If you think Dianetics is for suckers, then this is the book for you.

Brainwashing is the use of indirect means to manipulate people to do what you want, while maintaining the illusion of free will. This can be as elegant as the gradual creation of a false reality, or as brutal as a cricket bat to the skull. The key element is that the subject doesn't know that he or she is being controlled, or at least not by whom.

Brainwashing as we know it today was developed during the Cold War, the Renaissance of human cruelty, because somehow hydrogen bombs, nerve gas, and weaponized anthrax weren't enough.

Over the years, brainwashing has only become more innovative and advanced in its outreach. Today, brainwashing influences everything from advertising to a commander in Afghanistan ordering a "psychological operations" team to manipulate U.S. senators. Everyday lunatics suddenly have a way to turn their own private madness into their own unpopular little religions, still obnoxious but now tax-exempt. That pesky Betty Friedan convinced America's women that they were bored at home and would have more fun changing their dress shields and swapping Bundt cake recipes at the *office* than at home around the daiquiri pitcher. And, bored with actually having to argue their products' benefits, advertisers now incorporate subliminal messages into mass media, prompting the phrase, "What is it about David Schwimmer that makes me want Taco Bell?"

With so many different options for your brainwashing needs, you need a little more direction than the "you're getting very sleepy" cliché. With a helpful icon for each brainwashing technique (see "How to Use This Book" that follows), *Brainwashing for Beginners* is the guide to assure you're the brainwasher, not the brainwashee.

HOW TO USE THIS BOOK

Brainwashing is a lot like sex: There are a lot of ways to do it, but some are messier than others. For clarity and convenience, we've outlined the most common techniques below and matched each with an icon that will appear when this approach is used throughout the book. We've used the most ideal techniques for each specific scenario that we've hypothesized, but make sure to look back at these techniques from time to time so you're not confusing love-bombing with destabilization. That would be awkward and hard to explain to the police.

CLASSICAL CONDITIONING

Classical conditioning is based on the theories of Russian researcher Ivan Petrovich Pavlov, who regularly fed his dogs at the ringing of a bell. Eventually the dogs would salivate at the sound of the bell regardless of whether food was present. Classical conditioning trains people to associate two previously unassociated things. For example, if you always get ice cream during *Designing Women*, you'll learn to love Delta Burke; but if you get an electric shock during *M*A*S*H*, you'll learn to hate and fear Alan Alda.

LUDOVICO TECHNIQUE

A re-education process used in Anthony Burgess's novel *A Clockwork Orange*. The Ludovico Technique exposes the subject to a certain stimulus ad nauseam, until they are horrified at the very concept of said stimulus. For example, if your roommate won't stop listening to old Spice Girls CDs, lock him in the basement and play "2 Become 1" for a few days. When he comes out, he won't even be able to look at a Union Jack without vomiting.

GASLIGHTING/MIND GAMES

Gaslighting is based on a technique used in the 1944 movie *Gaslight* where Charles Boyer convinces Ingrid Bergman that she's losing her mind by manipulating her surroundings. From this it has come to mean any attempt to make the subject doubt the evidence of his or her own senses and then take advantage of the resulting confusion.

SUBLIMINAL MESSAGES/HYPNOSIS

Subliminal messages are coercive messages concealed in a larger work that are designed to influence behavior without the subject even noticing them. Hypnosis is planting ideas while a subject is in a suggestible trance state. It got you to buy Coke and it'll get you to shut up.

PROJECT MK-ULTRA

An illegal CIA research program where the U.S. government altered an individual's mental state with drugs, alcohol, other chemicals, etcetera, to make them receptive to manipulation.

Four martinis and you won't be able to turn down your friend's invitation to help paint a community mural—"for the kids!"

LOVE-BOMBING

Sugar doesn't just overwhelm diabetics. Love-bombing is a technique commonly used by cult recruiters, and by abusers in the early stages of romantic relationships where you inundate an individual with affection and signs of friendship until they will do anything you say.

ABUSE/TORTURE

It's not graceful, it's not legal, and it's not elegant, but it *is* effective.

DESTABILIZATION

Making sure that no aspect of the subject's life is stable or reliable. If everything is in flux, the subject will cling to the only stable thing they can find, whether that be UC–Boulder's Hillel or an abusive boyfriend named Clarence who trains show reptiles.

PROPAGANDA

False or exaggerated information disseminated to shape public perception. Technically distinct from advertising, but not by much.

Brainwashing isn't a country club; you don't have to be wealthy, successful, or even white to manipulate those around you. All you need is determination, moral bankruptcy, and this book. Since you clearly already have the latter, it's time to turn the page, cast your scruples aside, and start making the world your own!

CHAPTER 1

MAKING WORK WORK FOR YOU

MANIPULATION AROUND THE OFFICE

There are many different avenues you can take to get ahead at the office. Some people are lucky enough to be born a Carrington-Colby-Dexter and use their family connections; some use a set of Lee press-ons, a water bra, and a can-do attitude to "romance" the boss; and others—God bless their hearts—actually show up to work on time and do their jobs well. If you were unfortunate enough to be born a Flotsky with a flat chest, and mornings just aren't your "thing," take heart. You can always use mind control to get that promotion. (Hell, it worked for Oprah.)

Objective #1: Trade-In for a Better Office

You have nothing against Janine personally—although it is a little tiring how she continually cuts *Broom Hilda* cartoons out from the paper and sticks them to the office refrigerator—it's just that she has a wonderful office. The east-facing windows provide plentiful morning sunshine for her assortment of miniature cacti, while your ferns waste away in your dim, north-facing shoebox. Janine's office is located directly over Subway, so she's greeted every morning with the reassuring aroma of five specialty breads. Your office faces an alley where the esteemed sandwich artists discard last week's imitation seafood salad. Janine's office neighbor is Ruth, the maternal secretary with the dish of assorted hard candies on her desk and a smile as warm as her crocheted sweater. Your neighbor is Larry, who wants to talk about his divorce if you have a minute; his wife never did. You could handle the listless plants and the moldering "crab," but you'll lose your mind if you have to overhear Larry on the phone one more time yelling, "You bitch! I get the kids for Purim! *I'm the Jewish one!*" You could wait for Janine to retire, or you could do something a little more underhanded.

Option 1.1: Scare Her Out

GASLIGHTING/MIND GAMES

And your mother said watching all four *House of Night* movies in a day wouldn't help you in the "real world!" Turn Janine's office into her own little six-by-eight Amityville and make her ask you to trade offices with her and protect her from the "ghosts." Use jam to create a worrying stain that keeps reappearing—and spreading. Poison her plants so there's a general atmosphere of "not thriving." Hide a small boombox in her air duct that quietly constantly plays a tape of scary Halloween sounds. Invest in a cane that would make Howard "Sandman" Sims jealous and continually slam her door shut from a distance—she'll know it's not the wind and it's certainly not "Showtime at the Apollo." If you have the technical know-how or a nerdy teenage son, give her computer a virus that causes the screen to go black, except for the continually scrolling, "I thirst I thirst I thirst." As her nerves fray and everyone else refuses to trade offices with her, be gallant and swap, declaring that you "ain't afraid of no ghosts." When she comes back a few days later to ask how you're getting on, nonchalantly say, "Oh, I just opened the windows and gave it a good airing. Cleared right up."

BEHAVIOR MODIFICATION TECHNIQUE: OTHER THINGS THAT MIGHT MAKE A HAUNTING "CLEAR RIGHT UP"

- A bowl of water (it said it was thirsty)
- A fine dusting of seasoned salt
- A good, strong dose of Febreze
- Playing the same Sammy Hagar song over and over again

Option 1.2: Romance Her Out

LOVE-BOMBING

Through forged notes and a careful priming of the rumor mill, encourage a midlife romance between Janine and Larry. If it gets schmaltzy enough, she'll timidly ask if you'll trade offices with her so she can be by her Larry-Bear.

Objective #2: Get a Raise

Ever since the economy pliéd its way off stage and directly into the orchestra pit, raises in your office have become a delightfully retro thing of the past, like drinking bourbon at 11 o'clock in the morning, or grabbing your secretary's ass as a way to say, "Now that's what I call a *pencil skirt!*" You understand that everyone has to make sacrifices while the stage hands attempt to fish the economy out of a French horn, but it doesn't make it any easier to be told, "If we had the money, you'd be the first person to get a raise this year," by your boss. It's such a tease. It's like the prettiest girl in the school telling you, "If Bobby hadn't asked me yesterday, I would have *totally* gone to the prom with you!" Oh yeah? Well, shoulda, woulda, coulda, sister, because come prom night, Bobby's going to be discovering the wild and wonderful world of third base while you sit in an empty parking lot drinking Schlitz and listening to "Since U Been Gone" on repeat. Likewise, you're three months late on your car payment, and Volkswagen doesn't accept earnest pats on the back or fifteen-dollar gift certificates to iTunes as payment for your Jetta. If your boss has made it clear that he's not going to give you a raise, it's time to change his mind for him.

Option 2.1: Show Him What He'd Be Missing
`DESTABILIZATION`

You know how you're always saying that the office would fall apart without you? Well, let it. Cash in your vacation, take a few weeks off, and place a framed picture of the popular 1960s band Herman's Hermits on your desk as your temp. Enjoy sleeping in and catching up on *The X-Files* reruns while your boss furiously googles "toner" and wonders why the Hermits aren't responding to his e-mails. It should take all of six hours until his world breaks down completely and he e-mails HR about the quickest way to fire those hippie "mop tops" and give you a raise.

Option 2.2: Make Him Think You're Straight-Up Poor

SUBLIMINAL MESSAGES/HYPNOSIS

Replace your normally well-pressed Men's Wearhouse suits with tattered rags and fingerless gloves, and spend your lunch breaks in front of the vending machine meekly asking your coworkers for "alms for the poor." Start referring to your superiors exclusively as "Gov'nahs." Hell, maybe even bribe a cop to chase you through the office while screaming, "Get back here, you *scamp!*" and twirling his billy club. Next time your boss is sittin' pretty in his Mazda Protégé en route to a Sizzler dinner, it'll be all he can do to not picture his favorite employee selling crushed daisies in the street to make ends meet. At that point he'll either give you a raise or adopt you. You win either way.

PARAPHERNALIA: OTHER FORMS OF COMPENSATION YOUR BOSS HAS PURSUED

- A stress ball that says "Don't worry, be happy!" that burst
- A beer koozie boasting, "I've got a case of the Mondays!"
- A year's subscription to *Prevention* magazine
- A gift certificate for five free guitar lessons
- A pep talk

Objective #3: Get Your Persistent Coworker to Stop Asking You Out

Some good office flirtation can be just what the doctor ordered to spice up the monotony of daily nine-to-five life. Suddenly you wake up in the morning and instead of contemplating a career in "air hosting" for forty-five minutes, you jump out of bed, eager to get to the office and see your work crush. More and more you find yourself actually *bathing* before work and not just throwing your hair under a beret, dousing yourself in Febreze, and calling it "hygiene." *Bad* office flirtation, however, can be the thing keeping you in bed wondering which airline has the most ass-masking uniforms. There's nothing more awkward than that guy in your office who won't stop asking you out. You've said no, you've told him you're seeing someone, you've made your desktop background a picture of you hugging your brother at your cousin's wedding and stare lovingly at it every time the guy walks by, but he still manages to work an uncomfortable invitation to dinner into all of your interactions. If you want his advances to stop but don't want to make things even more awkward by inviting HR to the party, it's up to you to brainwash him into thinking that he can do better.

Option 3.1: Use Reverse Psychology

LOVE-BOMBING

If you're anything like us, you tend to develop crushes on people, find out that the feeling is mutual, and are immediately less interested in them. Who knows why it happens? It probably has something to do with secret self-esteem issues and being latchkey kids, but the point is that you can use this to your advantage. Bombard him with romantic advances, shower him with praise, harass him about getting together—anything to tap into his subconscious and make him think the thrill is gone.

Option 3.2: Every Time He Asks You Out, Blow an Air Horn in His Face

CLASSICAL CONDITIONING

Have you ever been to a high-school basketball game? Christ, those air-horn things are abrasive. After a few blasts to the ear, it might be enough to make him stop talking to you *altogether*.

EQUIPMENT: OTHER THINGS YOU CAN BLARE

- A rape whistle
- A B-flat clarinet
- The fire alarm
- A foghorn
- A novelty car horn that plays "La Cucaracha"

Objective #4: Get the IT Department to Give You Unfiltered Internet Access

You don't appreciate the tight leash that the IT department keeps you on. You can get online, sure, but the only websites you can access without Chris Hansen showing up at your cubicle "door" with a pitcher of iced tea and two Florida state troopers are IBM.com and an online calculator. Drafting a work e-mail is like spending a weekend at your girlfriend's uncomfortably religious parents' house: You go to painstaking efforts to say "heck" instead of "hell" and find yourself mindlessly talking about pleasant weather patterns to avoid involving yourself in anything that could be misconstrued as inappropriate. One time you slipped and e-mailed your mother to thank her for the tickets to *Damn Yankees* and ended up in a three-hour-long HR seminar on the ethical use of company technology. God forbid you have to use "come" and "titmouse" in the same sentence or your computer would explode. While it's understandable that companies don't want their employees dicking around on the Internet all day, it's also unclear what they expect you to do if you're *not*. When you're only given about an hour of real work to do in a day, it's easy for the other seven to quickly fill up with "miscellaneous" tasks, like diagnosing yourself with lupus on WebMD or getting in a bidding war for pogs on eBay. If you don't want your boss to "challenge" you with more work but the nerds in IT refuse to bend the rules and help you out, you can always rely on manipulation to get the job done.

Option 4.1: Throw a Kegger in the IT Nerds' Office

ABUSE/TORTURE

When the nerds leave their lair to tend to the "wireless printer emergency" you called in on the fourth floor, roll in a couple of cold kegs, fill up the room with that year's rowdy summer interns, throw on a Black Eyed Peas mix, and turn that shit up to eleven. When the nerds come back and demand that you leave their office, restart "My Humps" and shout, "Who wants to do a body shot?" When they realize that you've spiked their Mountain Dew with grain alcohol and replaced their inhalers with whip-its, they'll be *begging* you to make a deal.

Option 4.2: Make Men Out of Them

`LOVE-BOMBING`

Fact: chances are none of these individuals has ever touched a human breast before. Is a tit-grab worth unlimited access to IMDb all day, every day? I leave that up to you and your God.

> ### OTHER PLAYS YOU CAN'T REFERENCE IN E-MAILS AT WORK
>
> - *The Best Little Whorehouse in Texas*
> - *The Vagina Monologues*
> - *Raunchy Asian Women*
> - *Puppetry of the Penis*
> - *Something Wicked This Way Comes*

Objective #5: Get a Company Car

There's a reason why bright-eyed and bushy-tailed college seniors find the prospect of soon being part of the workforce so glamorous: the corporate perks. When you're twenty-two years old, living in a basement, and relying on stolen dining-hall waffles and jugs of Powerade to sustain your life, being given a free Blackberry is like someone handing you the keys to the Free Sex and Lobster Shop. Veterans of the workforce, however, know better. The occasional free business lunch is nice, but you have to sit through a *business lunch* to get one. A free membership to the company gym is cool, but it also means that everyone sees you sweat profusely as you struggle to keep up the brisk walking pace of the pregnant woman on the treadmill next to you. That being said, there's one corporate perk coveted by everyone in the office from the most jaded executive to the lowliest junior associate: a company car. You know why? Because it's a car. That you got for *free*. It's like you won *The Price Is Right* and didn't even have to guess the price of a grandfather clock to do it. Unfortunately, most companies don't hand out company cars to just any old research assistant that strolls into their boss's office asking for one, so you're going to have to manipulate your boss into thinking you're more worthy than you probably are.

Option 5.1: Every Time You See Your Boss, Tell Him You're Running Late to a Squash Game with a Client

CLASSICAL CONDITIONING

This might be an incredibly dated social ritual from 1980s movies like *Trading Places* and old episodes of *Dynasty*, but high-powered business executives seem like they are always networking over games of squash. So whenever you see your boss, just act frazzled and tell him you can't talk because you're horribly late to play squash with [insert prospective client here] and *oof*, you hope the cross-town bus gets you there in time.

Option 5.2: Suck Up to Him Mercilessly

LOVE-BOMBING

It worked with your dad for your sweet sixteen and it certainly can't hurt now. (That being said, depending on what genders and lifestyles are in play, you should be hesitant to hang on your boss's shoulder and tell him he's the "best daddy ever." As it turns out, that has two meanings in certain cultures and HR is not easily amused.)

CRIB SHEET: PRICES OF COMMON *THE PRICE IS RIGHT* ITEMS

- Bottle of Garlique: $15.99
- Bottle of Mrs. Dash: $2.99
- Dr. Scholl's Massaging Gel Insoles: $9.00
- Children's Motrin: $9.99
- Tube of Icy Hot cream: $7.29

Objective #6: Recover from a Major Office Fuckup

Look, nobody's perfect. It's why pencils have erasers, cars have insurance, and Catholics have annulments. Everyone makes a mistake every now and then and it's just proof that we're all human. Or at least that's what you keep telling yourself as you vomit in the ladies' bathroom because you just realized you accidentally sent an e-mail saying, "Dude, not to be racist, but why are Asian people *always* carrying plastic bags?" to your entire company. (Although to be fair, "Allie" is absurdly close to "All" in your address book and the mice in this office are *touchy*.) Okay, take a deep breath. It's not the end of the world: (1) You raised an interesting point, and (2) there's a good chance that nobody even had time to read it. Nope. Nope, we take that back; your boss just sent you an e-mail asking you to come see him in his office immediately. Well, maybe it's about something else? Nope. The subject is very clearly "RE: Doesn't JanSport have a Hong Kong office?" Yeah, this isn't good. But it doesn't necessarily mean that you're about to get fired either. Remember that it's anyone's game when you know how to brainwash and your boss wants to talk to you behind closed doors.

Option 6.1: Drug Your Way out of an Uncomfortable Conversation

PROJECT MK-ULTRA

Slip three Benadryl pills into your boss's coffee when he isn't looking and wait for him to conk out mid-confrontation. Hang out in his office playing Snood on your phone for a while, and then emerge an hour later with tears running down your face so your coworkers think you just got the talking-to of your life. When you get back to your desk, send your boss an e-mail thanking him for the second chance and attach the 500-word essay on a time in your life when you felt stereotyped that he "requested." Your boss will be confused when he wakes up, but odds are he'll assume he just passed out in a fit of rage and you got what you deserved. Yeah, it sucks that you actually have to write a 500-word essay on a time in your life when you felt stereotyped, but then again, you know, that *was* a pretty racist e-mail.

FOR YOUR FILES: EXCERPT FROM YOUR MOVING ESSAY ABOUT BEING STEREOTYPED

"I guess I knew I was different on my first day of kindergarten. I was so excited to make new friends, but once the other children saw my flowing blonde hair, sparkling blue eyes, and pert button nose, they sneered, 'We don't want to play with *you*, you look stuck up!' I didn't know it then, but this wouldn't be the first time in my life when people would assume I'm a bad person because I'm so very pretty. *Far from*."

Option 6.2: Rely on an Absurd Mind-Fuck

GASLIGHTING/MIND GAMES

If it's the fourth down with five seconds on the clock and your career is on the line, go ahead and throw that Hail Mary: Tell him you were being ironic because *you're* Asian and get offended when he tries to tell you otherwise. If you do this well, he'll start doubting himself after a while and justifying that you might be from that steppe area where Eastern Europe meets Mongolia, and is that heavy eyeliner or genetics? If you can work out a few tears or a story about your relatives being in a Japanese internment camp, you might even get promoted.

Objective #7: Get Reimbursed for a Frivolous Trip

With a little creativity, initiative, and brainwashing, nearly every vacation can be written off as a legitimate business expense, be it a beachside conference in Hawaii or something a little less standard. Let's say, for example, that you finally took the trip you've always dreamed of: a stop-by-stop recreation of Mötley Crüe's infamous heroin-and-whiskey-fueled 1987 tour of the Deep South. You rented a rusty 1979 Camaro, filled the trunk with several dozen bottles of whiskey, and tore across Dixie like a one-man Union army. It was perfect, even down to your wife, Sandy, agreeing to wear only tube tops and answer to the name "Cherry Tomato" for the duration of the trip. This idyll wasn't cheap, however; gas prices were still cartoonishly high, and Sandy insisted on staying in Holiday Inns or better since having seen a documentary about the various fluids travelers leave in cheaper lodgings

("... even Barbara Walters was disgusted, and she's seen everything!"). Instead of cutting back on luxuries and carefully budgeting until you recover financially, get a reimbursement from the boss via one of the methods below.

Option 7.1: Overwhelm Him with Techno Babble
PROPAGANDA

Now that technology changes every fifteen seconds, everyone is afraid of being left behind and missing the next allegedly innovative "platform." Explain to your boss that you were "spearheading an advanced flash-mob viral marketing burst fact-finding excursion to traditionally underserved areas." This means that you went to some hick towns and started some fights, but it has enough modern, marketing-sounding words that your boss will likely approve the expenses in order not to seem behind the times.

Option 7.2: Get Him on Your Side
CLASSICAL CONDITIONING

Every time something good happens for your boss, play Mötley Crüe. He gets a raise? "Smokin' in the Boys Room." He gets a pretty new secretary? "Girls, Girls, Girls." The SEC calls off its investigation? "Dr. Feelgood." Eventually, he'll be as big a fan as you are, and he'll sign off on your reimbursement forms with a merry laugh and that phrase, "Aw, man. Wish I'd been there." You can transfer this method to other trips; just identify a key element of your planned vacation, and always bring that up when your boss is doing well so he associates it with good feelings. You'll have to plan a year or more in advance, but it will be worth the trouble to go for free.

**COMPARISON SHOPPING: ROAD TRIPS
THAT ARE LESS FUN TO RE-ENACT**

- Barbarian crossing of the frozen Rhine (405–406)
- Napoleon's winter invasion of Russia (1812)
- O. J. Simpson's white Bronco escapade (1994)
- Driving to your mother's house to have lunch with her and Dan, then to your father's house to have dinner with him and Madge (every damn Thanksgiving since the divorce)

Objective #8: Convince the Boss to Let You Work from Home

Compare, if you will, working a day at the office to working a day from home. To work at the office, you have to get up early, put on pants, commute, eat whatever's convenient near your building, and make small talk with coworkers. To work from home, however, you can get up later, enjoy complete freedom whether or not to don a pant item, commute by going into the other room, make yourself a Cobb salad in your own kitchen for lunch, and if you want to hear mindless yammering you can turn on *Press Your Luck*. Thanks to technology, going to the office is rapidly becoming outdated; the only thing keeping everyone except janitors and the police from working at home is that most companies fear a loss of productivity and corporate prestige if all their employees suddenly begin doing their work while eating a slice of avocado with their fingers and yelling "No whammies, no whammies, no whammies, *argh!*" at the television. Sorry, kids, but that's the boss man's problem. If he wants the company to seem fancy, he can add a ship's wheel to the logo. Meanwhile, it's a fair argument that you're more productive *watching The Young and the Restless* than *wondering* about it at your desk. Use one of these techniques to stay at home but off the unemployment rolls.

Option 8.1: The Global Warming Debate

PROPAGANDA

"Greening" is a good way to score some cheap points. Explain to your boss that, since you won't be driving to work or using the office machines, the company's "carbon footprint" will be reduced by letting you work from home. Make sure to pepper your presentation with pictures of wistful-looking polar bears and flooded Third World villages. He probably won't care, but someone on the board of directors probably will. If he can pitch your staying at home as environmental activism, he stands to get a little kudos—and you stand to catch up on *General Hospital*.

Option 8.2: Ruin Everyone's Day

ABUSE/TORTURE

Be the darkest little rain cloud you can be. Steer every conversation to death, decay, decline, despair, dejection, and dismay. If you can make the general atmosphere of the office bleak enough, your boss may instruct you to work from home so that the general mood will lighten and he can get some work done instead of sitting in his darkened office, staring at a picture of his wife and pondering the inexorable passage of time. Or he'll get so depressed he doesn't *care* where you are, and either way . . .

SIGNS OF SUCCESS: OTHER THINGS YOUR BOSS HAS BEGUN DOING BECAUSE HE'S SO DEPRESSED

- Embracing his children tightly and telling them not to repeat his mistakes
- Asking his wife to slap him during sex "so he can feel something, anything"
- Staring blankly into the middle distance
- Drinking while paging slowly through his high-school yearbook and thinking about how many of his classmates have died
- Weeping

Objective #9: Get Your Office to Stock "Full Flavor" Sodas

Congratulations. You finished puberty and got your GED. You're an adult now. Now armed with pubic hair and a shaky understanding of how checks and balances work, you're ready to join the grown-up world, which largely entails endless worry. At night, when sleep doesn't come, you'll have plenty to occupy your mind: your credit score, your retirement savings, your house's assessed value, and the famed bugbear of a man's middle years, the prostate: the Little Gland That Could, Until It Couldn't, and I Don't Want to Talk to the Doctor About It Because He'll Want to Feel It, but Oh God, What If It's Cancer? Fortunately, the powers that be at your office know that you're worried, so they've decided to take a difficult decision off your hands by offering only diet soda and water at meetings and in vending machines. How *considerate*. Here you were, paralyzed by the choices, and they've lifted the cross from your shoulders like a *Fortune* 500 Simon of Cyrene. The national economy is in tatters, terrorists are on Facebook, and you felt a *distinct twinge* in your prostate this morning, but huzzah! Some corporate nursemaid has helped you postpone diabetes for fifteen minutes! No, thank you. You can make your own decisions. Get the sugar sodas back with one of these tricks.

Option 9.1: Nausea

`PROJECT MK-ULTRA`

Put just the *tiniest* bit of syrup of ipecac into everyone's diet sodas when the opportunity presents itself. Your goal here is not to cause an office-wide barf-athon but to cause mild to moderate discomfort. Do it enough times, and everyone in the office will associate diet sodas with the internal monologue, "Oh, I might *actually vomit.* Okay, it's going away. . . . *Wait. No.* Okay. If I have to, I can throw up in the recycle bin, and then . . . wipe my mouth with my pantyhose or something. I must be getting older. I used to be able to drink seventeen sodas a day, but now . . . maybe it's something in the diet ones?" Do this to enough people, and hopefully one of them will have the strings to pull to get real sodas back in the office.

Option 9.2: Internet Cranks

`PROPAGANDA`

What is so wonderful about the Internet is that so many lunatics have access to it. The Internet is full of wild claims and conspiracy theories: somewhere in among "camel milk cures autism" and "Barack Obama was born in the U.S.A., but to a trained seal named Claudia Whiskers," you can find a carefully crafted, well-argued,

completely untrue series of essays about how artificial sweeten-
ers are an EU/UN plot to cause homosexuality, insanity, and fallen
arches. Download these essays, tack on a respectable-looking
logo, add a *Dilbert* strip to the top so it looks legit, and send them
as an interoffice chain letter. They'll open it for the *Dilbert*; they'll
read on because of the wild accusations. And since no one wants
to be an unstable Nancy with flat feet, they'll take action.

KNOW THE TERRAIN: OTHER THINGS THE INTERNET IS CONVINCED OF

- The ghost of Colonel Sanders has cursed a Japanese baseball team
- Donna Reed knew who killed JFK, but she remained silent to "let the country heal"
- Ronald Reagan was reincarnated in Tibet and may become a lama
- There's always room for another pretentious indie music blog
- Nothing is funnier than a fat child falling down

Objective #10: Enslave Your Assistant

Once you reach a certain level in your career, you may wind up
with an assistant. In theory, this person exists to help you manage
your work responsibilities: scheduling meetings, organizing files,
making calls when you just can't face talking to that pompous
prick in accounting yourself, putting just enough Irish cream into
your coffee that you glide through the budget meeting but not *so*
much that you get tipsy and punctuate the inevitable PowerPoint
slideshow with armpit farts. A good assistant is worth his weight

in gold; a *great* assistant is literally priceless, assuming that they develop such a fanatical loyalty to you that they work for high-fives and live by foraging off the bagel tray. As nice as it is having someone clear your path at the office, what's really grand is having them take care of your home life as well. Want a formal English garden installed in the backyard? Need someone to make love to your wife if you're too bloated from eating six chilidogs as part of a show of virility to impress a potential investor? Tired of tying your own damn shoes every day like a chump? Make your assistant fill these less strictly professional needs by using one of the methods below.

Option 10.1: *Carthago Delenda Est*
DESTABILIZATION

Without letting your assistant know you're behind it, knock down everything in his life except his work relationship with you. Intercept his rent payment so he gets evicted and his credit suffers. Hire a big dumb "actor slash model" to seduce away his girl-friend. Forge a letter from his parents explaining that they're *terribly* sorry, but he was a mistake, and to avoid further awkwardness it might be best to part ways. Each time a pillar of his life falls, he'll draw closer to you—and eventually you'll be all that's left. Dazed, he'll be eager to do anything to preserve his narrowing island of stability.

Option 10.2: Feed Him Pufferfish
PROJECT MK-ULTRA

During the 1980s, Wade Davis, an ethnobotanist from Harvard, published work arguing that the myth of Haitian zombies came from an actual practice in which people were dosed with pufferfish poison and a native hallucinogenic plant to make them disoriented, obedient servants with no volition. It's not the most convincing story ever, but it is pretty cool if it works. You may have to substitute street-corner LSD for the native plant, but you can probably buy spare pufferfish parts from a well-connected busboy at an upscale Japanese restaurant. Slip 'em both in his latte and see where it goes.

EQUIPMENT CHECKLIST: OTHER THINGS YOU CAN BUY FROM THAT BUSBOY

- Kidneys (assorted)
- "Gucci" sneakers
- A Botox-like substance
- Black-market DVDs of low-budget Chinese historical epics
- A "Sønÿ" camcorder
- Diabetic testing strips

Objective #11: Convince an Employee to Retire

Gert is a nice lady, but she's getting on in years, and it might be time for her to slow down. You can't quite pin down how old she is: Her Social Security number has eight digits, and once in a moment of candor she let slip that her first job was as an army nurse during the war . . . against Spain. You've tried to gently drop hints about "the autumn years" and how nice it would be to spend all day watching BBC-produced Miss Marple mysteries, but she just laughs and says she'd be embarrassed if the Lord came for her and she was goofing off. An admirable sentiment, but Gert is really no longer prepared for the modern working world: She continues to refer to her computer as the "deluxe telegraph," and once gave a deeply odd presentation titled "Austria-Hungary, Abyssinia, and the Ottoman Empire: Today's Emerging Markets." It's time for some new blood; specifically, new blood that doesn't expect to be paid in gold Liberty dollars. You'll have to be careful, but you can get Gert to leave of what she will believe is her own free will.

Option 11.1: The End of an Era

GASLIGHTING/MIND GAMES

With any luck, your other employees are as tired as you are of hearing Gert talk about how tacky Grace Coolidge was, so it should be easy to enlist their help pretending that the business has gone bankrupt. Arrange for everyone to be absent or quietly crying when Gert arrives. Explain to Gert that the old firm is bust, gone, over, kaput! Mutter vague things about how you'll have to go live in a Hooverville. She'll be sad, but you'll be speaking her language.

Option 11.2: And the Murderer Is . . .

LUDOVICO TECHNIQUE

Dress as a burglar, tie Gert to her chair, and force her to watch every single Miss Marple mystery, but shut each one off before the killer's identity is revealed. If it's a long weekend and you have no plans, play them over two or three times. By the end of this ordeal, Gert will be consumed with such a desperate need to know who killed everyone and why and how and when and where that she may well give notice right away, the sooner to get home and bring these shows up on the light box. Depending on your target, you can use any mystery show—or mix and match, so they'll have to watch season after season of multiple shows to find the answers.

KNOW YOUR MATERIALS: THE MOST NERVE-RACKING TV CLIFFHANGERS

- "Who Shot J. R. Ewing?" on *Dallas*
- "Who Shot Mr. Burns?" on *The Simpsons*
- Jessica Fletcher is locked in an Irish castle with rats and a skeleton on *Murder, She Wrote*
- Is Jessica Tate really dead? on *Soap*
- The Moldavian massacre on *Dynasty*

CHAPTER 2

BE THE MARY, NOT THE RHODA

TOWARD MORE OBEDIENT FRIENDS

Bernice K. Larch, CPA, has been your best friend ever since that fateful day you signed up for an evening pottery class at The Learning Annex. Who knew that when you chose the workstation next to the snarky divorcee with a long, grey braid that a lifelong friendship would develop over the pinch pots? Bernice has been there for you through thick and thin. She taught you how to substitute Splenda for sugar in a guilt-free recipe for Seven Deadly Layers Chocolate Sin Cake; she opened you up to the no-holds-barred world of country-western line dancing; and she even volunteered to be the designated driver for Maryland Deathfest IX when you were going through a Pantera phase. But even Bernice K. Larch, CPA, has to draw the line somewhere. And she draws it right before giving you an enema because you can't hold the hose, hand mirror, and someone's hand all at the same time. If Bernice is being as resolute as your impacted bowels, it's time to use a little manipulation to get things moving along.

Objective #12: Get Your Friend to Stop Wearing That Embarrassing Thing in Public

Unless you've lived your entire life as a nudist, mime, or member of the Blue Man Group, odds are you've been a fashion victim once or twice in your time. When trends change faster than a stripper between sets, how could you not? Once upon a time, a jester hat and a Stussy T-shirt were considered to be cutting-edge street fashion. Now they just remind everyone that you spent 1996 being *not* sexually active. Trends can seem like a good idea at the time, but then you find yourself flipping through your cousin's wedding album twelve years later wondering why in a ballroom of 500 people, not one person had the balls to tell you that you don't have the bone structure to pull off gold lamé culottes. Which is exactly why you've spent the last six months trying to get your friend to stop constantly wearing that ironic John Deere baby tee. First of all, it's not even ironic; it's just ill fitting. Second, just stop. And that should be enough. It's hard to imagine being attracted to anything to the point where you can't hear your friends telling you what a jackass you look like, nevertheless a piece of *tractor paraphernalia*. If you're tired of walking down the street and being the friend of "That Girl," brainwash her into sharing the "irony" with the Goodwill bin.

Option 12.1: Douse It in Pheromones to Attract the Wrong Sex

PROJECT MK-ULTRA

When the only advances you receive are round after round of free boilermakers from "Shawna by the pool tables" and a barrage of invitations to next month's k.d. lang concert, it's tempting to take a long, hard look in the mirror and wonder if the problem doesn't start at home.

Option 12.2: Stealthily Outfit It with an Anti-Theft Censor

CLASSICAL CONDITIONING

After the third Old Navy manager asks her to drop her bags and assume the position, she'll start associating her favorite baby tee with abrasive beeping and a pat-down from Darrell's security wand and not redneck irony.

FOR YOUR REFERENCE: OTHER ITEMS IN YOUR FRIEND'S GOODWILL BAG

- A pair of JNCO jeans
- Oversized decorative belt
- Board shorts
- A pair of Airwalks
- A deep V-neck T-shirt with "BATTLE ROYALE" in silver letters
- A faux vintage T-shirt that says "Gettin' Lucky in Kentucky"
- A monogrammed terrycloth track suit

Objective #13: Get Your Friends to Overeat So You're the "Thin One"

Every group of friends has a similar set of archetypes: There's the Smart One (the professor from *Gilligan's Island*, Simon from *Alvin and the Chipmunks*); the Hot One (Joey Tribbiani from *Friends*, Blanche Devereaux from *The Golden Girls*); the Endearing Asshole (Cordelia Chase on *Buffy the Vampire Slayer*, Archie Bunker from *All in the Family*); the Funny Fat One (Norm Peterson from *Cheers*, Suzanne Sugarbaker from *Designing Women*); and the Wacky Ethnic/Gay/Other Bonus Round (Mac Robinson on *Night Court*, Enrique "Ricky" Vasquez on *My So-Called Life*, which hits a gay/ ethnic double down). You've come to realize that in your group of friends, you've been pigeonholed as the Funny Fat One. Problem is, despite your "diabetes chic physique," not one of the big bones in your body is funny. No matter how many weekend workshops you register for at The Second City, you still have the comedic tim-ing of a dead piglet. It's become embarrassing; people keep turn-ing to you for a zany quip but your mouth is always full of jalapeno poppers. If you're just not funny and have a Garfield-esque reac-tion to diets, the next best thing is to pork up your friends so you have a shot at Smart One or Asshole.

Option 13.1: Inundate Your Friends with Goodies

LOVE-BOMBING

You can't tell a good Helen Keller joke to save your life, but you *did* learn to cook from your Louisiana-born grandmother who couldn't make ice water without adding lard. Every time you see your friends, bring a platter of twice-fried butter and sugar pie. Unhealthy sweets like these are as addictive as they are fattening, and before your friends know it they'll be eating frozen biscuits right out of the tin (provided their pudgy little fingers can still open the tube) and you'll be a toothpick in a bowl of olives.

FOOD POISONING: OTHER DISHES YOU LEARNED AT MEEMAW'S KNEE

- Bacon-wrapped bourbon balls
- Deep-fried French toast
- Red velvet cake with a lard swirl
- Ham-infused fried mozzarella
- Chicken-fried *everything*; also, she garnished mint juleps with a turkey leg

---

Option 13.2: Apply the Xanax Diet

PROJECT MK-ULTRA

Antidepressants are known for their side effects of weight gain and slow metabolisms. Obtain a prescription, mash up the pills, and put them in the saltshaker for your next dinner party. Or pass them out as vitamins. Or claim they're ecstasy. Whatever gets them down their gullets. Within a few months your friends will face their growing waistlines with an odd sense of optimism and calm.

Objective #14: Get a Friend to Be Your Permanent Designated Driver

There's nothing funny about drunk driving. It's stupid, dangerous, and can be avoided if you designate a driver at the beginning of the night to stay sober and get you and your friends home safely. That being said, actually *being* the DD is a drag. The benefit of potentially saving your friends' lives is almost negated by having to spend all night figuring out how to dance to techno music sober. Suddenly you're on the floor doing a very slow-moving worm and not because you're being ironic, but because a babysitter let you watch an episode of *Soul Train* once in 1985, and that and Don Cornelius's glasses are all that's coming back right now. You justify that it's okay to have one drink because you're 5'9" and just had a taco, but one drink becomes two, two become three, and suddenly you're swerving down the Jersey Turnpike making a deal with God that if He lets you and your friends get home in one piece, you'll stop masturbating for a month and never drink Everclear again. At a certain point it's just easier to manipulate one of your sucker friends into being DD *every* night with one of these techniques.

Option 14.1: Stage an Intervention and Get Them to Quit Drinking

GASLIGHTING/MIND GAMES

Gather a handful of family members, toss 'em in a room at the Red Roof Inn, and tell your friend to come to room 1111 for a sex toy party. When your friend shows up, horny and confused, sit her down and explain that you see a bunch of people in this room that love her like crazy, but you feel like you're losing her here. She'll cry and deny she has a problem, you'll read your letter saying that she does, you put the big hand in the little hand and *boom*—ninety days later she's back from Betty Ford and you have your official DD.

Option 14.2: Constantly Get Them Sick So They're Always on Antibiotics

PROJECT MK-ULTRA

Start collecting used tissues, tongue depressors, latex gloves, etcetera from the doctor's office and treat your friend's house like a giant petri dish. Polish the silverware with the tissues, scrub their toothbrush on the tongue depressors, put on the latex gloves and touch *everything*. Your friend won't be able to drink for ten days if they get put on antibiotics, which thankfully is *more* than enough time to get you to and from Bonnaroo.

FROM THE POLYGRAPH MACHINE: OTHER BROKEN PROMISES YOU'VE MADE TO GOD

- Pay your student loans on time
- Take a multivitamin every day
- Do volunteer work even when it's not court-ordered
- Get more fiber
- Never miss another Easter at church to stay home and watch *Office Space*

Objective #15: Get Your Friends to Throw You a Birthday Party

Being in charge of your own birthday plans is one of the more depressing aspects of becoming an adult, up there with having to factor haircuts into your budget. Birthdays are always awesome when you're a little kid because your parents are basically unpaid party planners for the first decade of your life, and all you have to do is show up to the party, eat some cake, try not to take your pants off, and cry for twenty minutes. Birthday parties in the second decade of your life are surprisingly similar to the first, except your parents aren't there to tell you to put your pants back on and strangers buy you alcohol. Then suddenly you're out of college and everything changes. Your birthday always falls on a Tuesday, you have to work late because nobody in the office gives a shit, and by the time you make it to happy hour with your friends, all you want to do is go home, take off your pants (at least some things never change), drink a bottle of wine, and fall asleep watching *Jeopardy!*. It's depressing. The only thing *more* depressing is being a grown-ass man who still needs his friends to make his birthday plans for him. Then again if you don't, you just end up spending another birthday depressed, drunk, and pantless with Alex Trebek. Obviously, the logical solution is to brainwash your friends into throwing you the best damn birthday party since you peed your pants while riding a rental elephant (23 was an awesome birthday).

Option 15.1: Kill Your Friends with Kindness

LOVE-BOMBING

Friendship is a two-way street. Maybe if you showed your friends how much you care about them, they'd be more likely to go out of their way and show you how much they care about you. Do chores for them that you know they hate. Tell them how nice they've been looking recently. Make them dinner one night just because. There's a pretty decent chance they might just think you're hitting on them, but even that's flattering in its own way.

Option 15.2: Fill Their Netflix Queues with Epic Party Movies

SUBLIMINAL MESSAGES/HYPNOSIS

You can't watch *Point Break* without trying to get your buddies to blow off work and go surfing (which is odd, considering you live in Topeka), so maybe after a few party movies, they'll want to throw one of their own in your honor.

GETTING THERE: OTHER UNCONVENTIONAL MODES OF TRANSPORTATION YOU'VE PEED YOUR PANTS ON

- The Chesapeake Bay water taxi
- A pogo stick
- Your cousin's thoroughbred horse, "Crisplin's Tuesday Morning"
- Airport shuttle at O'Hare
- A rainforest canopy zip-line in Costa Rica

Objective #16: Get Your Friend to Be the Shitty Half of a Halloween Costume

Halloween is how the calendar atones for shitty holidays like Tax Day and Yom Kippur. And you, sir, are *forgiven*. What isn't there to love about Halloween? It's a holiday dedicated to eating candy, getting drunk, and trying to have sex with as many Teenage Mutant Ninja Turtles as possible. When the crisp fall weather rolls in and e-vites for Halloween parties go out, friends all over the country pair up and sit down to think of that year's dual costume. Unfortunately, not every Power Ranger can be the pink one. For every Batman there's a Robin; for every Beauty there's a Beast; and for every Cher at the party, there's a girl named Heather begrudgingly dressed as Sonny Bono, desperately trying to make a crotch sock and a handlebar moustache look feminine. If you don't want your Halloween to be spent coyly twisting strands of a Mark Hamill wig around your finger while you recite fun facts about the great city of Palm Springs to a *very* disinterested Phantom of the Opera, brainwash your friend into taking the back seat this year with one of the following.

Option 16.1: Use a Spooky Prop to Hypnotize Them

SUBLIMINAL MESSAGES/HYPNOSIS

Nearly every Halloween decoration, be it ghost, witch, or spooky pumpkin, has creepy blinking lights for eyes. Go hog wild in the seasonal Halloween store and stock up. Use the many blinking lights to draw your friend into a trance and suggest that this year, you'll be the "silver fox" Anderson Cooper and she'll be the "beige gerbil" Rachel Maddow.

Option 16.2: Get Them Drunk

PROJECT MK-ULTRA

If there's anything more synonymous with Halloween than blinky-eyed ghost/witch/spooky pumpkin decorations, it's novelty seasonal pumpkin-flavored microbrews. Get your friend drunk on a case of Ichabod Crane's Headless Hops & Barley before you go out and she won't even know that she's wearing pants, let alone Steve Urkel high-waters, to compliment your Laura Winslow jumper.

POWER SHARING: DUAL COSTUMES WITHOUT A CLEAR WINNER OR LOSER

- Peaches and Herb
- Cagney and Lacey
- Starsky and Hutch
- A feminist and a vegan
- The Allman Brothers

Objective #17: Get a Friend to Go with You to an Embarrassing Concert

As far as elitist music snobs go, you're the most self-important, Brooklyn-dwelling, autoharp-playing, I-liked-Arcade-Fire-until-they-sold-out-and-played-the-Grammys blogging, Pitchforkiest friend of Mark Ronson at VICE's "Suicide and Labial Folds" release party. That being said, Sugar Ray plays some pretty goddamn good music. "Fly"? "Every Morning"? Or 2005's little-known "Psychedelic Bee"? All jewels in Sugar Ray's crown. And yet you buy *one* little fedora signed by Mark McGrath on eBay and suddenly nobody wants you on their podcasts anymore. Even your friends think you're kind of a douche bag, and the last concert they went to was Vampire Weekend. *Vampire Weekend!* Can you imagine?! What is this, 2008? What are we, Vassar undergrads? Mark McGrath would have appreciated that joke. Mark McGrath would have thrown his head back in laughter as the tips of his spiky blond hair caught the *Entertainment Tonight* studio lights and glistened like the pure blue waters of the Aegean Sea. Mark McGrath would have also agreed to accompany you to a Sugar Ray concert, which is more than any of your stupid "Oh-did-you-hear-about-this-cool-new-band-called-Len?" friends can say. You've got two backstage passes to a Sugar Ray concert next week and unless you manipulate one of your friends to come with you, you're screwed. Mark McGrath doesn't give his fedoras to *losers*.

Option 17.1: Play the Band's Music Whenever Your Friend Has Sex

CLASSICAL CONDITIONING

Lord knows you can't hear Morrissey's "Moondance" without feeling like you're right back in that Honda Spyder doin' it with the captain of the lacrosse team. Do it enough and they'll slowly start to associate the band's music with something positive, like sex, and not "Mark McGrath gargling a bag of dicks."

Option 17.2: Give the Band Fake Street Cred

GASLIGHTING/MIND GAMES

Did you know that Sugar Ray is supposedly making a huge comeback? Did you know that they produced Muse's new album and are headlining SXSW next year? Or that the *Los Angeles Times* did this really interesting profile on Mark McGrath and apparently he spent the better part of the early '00s addicted to poppers and hoarding? Well, that's because none of that is true. But your friend doesn't have to know that!

> ### LEVERAGE: MARK MCGRATH'S OTHER VICES FROM THE EARLY AUGHTS
>
> - Over-the-counter antihistamines
> - The light, escapist fiction of Danielle Steele
> - Choco-Tacos
> - Sun-In
> - Bra snapping

Objective #18: Get Your Friend to Stop Texting You Constantly

Not to get all Luddite, but there is a time and place for phone conversations. Relaxing on your deck with a glass of Shiraz and a bowl of pita chips, for example, is a great time to pick up the phone and have a long, newsy chat with a good friend. Sitting in the waiting room at your dermatologist's office, however, is not. In the latter, it's just genuinely easier to shoot a quick text to your friend saying, "Remember that semester we were really into pinochle? LOL," and be done with it, rather than have a huge conversation about how you can't really talk because you're at the dermatologist's waiting to get a mole with irregular borders looked at, but *remember when?* That being said, there is such a thing as over-texting. A text message might be the less invasive interruption when compared to a phone call, but it's an interruption nonetheless. Nobody wants to be woken up at three o'clock in the morning by a small symphony of text message alerts coming from your phone because your friend just got drunk and watched *Donnie Darko* for the first time and now he's got more questions than Wikipedia does answers. If at the end of the day he refuses to respect your text message boundaries, manipulate him into putting the phone down with one of these brainwashing techniques.

Option 18.1: Constantly Change His Text Alert to Something Embarrassing

`DESTABILIZATION`

When in doubt, a fart is usually the best way to go. It's timeless, elegant, jazzy. The key is to not give up when your friend inevitably changes his text alert back to its normal ding. Prank him over and over again until he's too paranoid to send a text message at all; God forbid he gets a delayed farty reply in the middle of Shabbat dinner. It's childish, but then again so is texting someone a play-by-play of the hot sauces at Hooter's because you're "bored as shit and want it written down somewhere for future reference."

Option 18.2: "Gift" Him a Jitterbug

`ABUSE/TORTURE`

Break his phone and replace it with one of those cell phones designed specifically for the elderly that can only send and receive phone calls and has a keypad the size of fucking Bahrain. Keep the complimentary book light for yourself though. You earned it.

FROM THE ARCHIVES: OTHER THINGS YOUR FRIEND HAS TEXTED TO YOU BECAUSE HE WANTS IT WRITTEN DOWN SOMEWHERE

- His locker combination at the gym
- This one stewardess' name
- His Hanukkah list
- Directions to the L train
- A picture of his penis that was meant for someone else

Objective #19: Get a Matching Tattoo with Your Best Friend

Getting a tattoo is a lot like homosexuality: It's not as taboo as it was fifty years ago, but that doesn't mean you can talk about it all day with your grandmother and still get your inheritance. Even though it seems like everyone these days has a tattoo, from Miley Cyrus to Meghan McCain ("Kucinich '08" in Olde English font; Republicans have to rebel, too), once upon a time they were only worn by the likes of sailors, bikers, and convicts. (And Polynesian warriors. But that was more of a shirts vs. skins kind of thing.) As a result, most offices still institute a "no visible tattoos" policy and your best friend's is apparently no different. If you've already left a nonrefundable down payment on your tattoo at the shop, but making a new best friend is too time-consuming, get her to roll up her sleeves with one of the following.

Option 19.1: Fake Your Death

GASLIGHTING/MIND GAMES

There are a thousand reasons to get a tattoo, but one of the most popular is to commemorate the death of a loved one. Fake your own death and hope that your memory lives on forever in the form of your best friend's new wrist tattoo. She might be pissed when she sees you in line for Soundgarden tickets a few days later, but it's easier to forgive and forget than to sit through eight sessions of laser tattoo removal.

SOCIAL RITUALS: OTHER WAYS YOUR FRIEND MOURNED YOUR DEATH

- Named a teddy bear after you
- Updated "Candle in the Wind" to be about you and sang it at karaoke night
- Held a candlelight vigil in your honor in the parking lot of Benihana
- Started a scholarship fund in your name at the local beauty academy
- Carved your name into her thigh

Option 19.2: Sign Her Up for the Navy

DESTABILIZATION

There's an old navy tradition where the night before a sailor deploys, she goes out and gets stewed, screwed, and tattooed. Sign her up for the Navy and join her in taking care of number three. In light of the circumstances, you'd also better go ahead and treat her to number one while you're at it. And as far as number two goes, what happened at field hockey camp stayed at field hockey camp, so do what feels right in the moment.

Objective #20: Get a Group of Friends Together to Go Camping

Truth be told, you made a pretty piss-poor Girl Scout during your two-year middle-school stint in Troop #1462. You wandered away from troop meetings in the church's multipurpose room to nosh on communion wafers, and faked a series of hysterical pregnancies to get out of overnight camping trips. Now that you're an adult, however, you finally understand how much fun camping can be. It combines all of your favorite activities (day drinking, outdoor drinking, repeatedly poking a fire with a long stick you found, an environment where people don't judge you for eating a hot dog after it falls on the ground, ghost stories) into one memory-making weekend. Unfortunately, your friends don't share your new outlook. Every time you try to rally the troops for a weekend getaway in the wilderness, all they hear is "bugs," "sleeping on the ground," "small chance someone will cut their way into your tent and turn your testicles into salt and pepper shakers," "no electricity," and automatically say no. Luckily for you, you're a master of manipulation.

Option 20.1: Slip Them a Psychedelic

PROJECT MK-ULTRA

According to every asshole stoner you've ever dated, psychedelic drugs like magic mushrooms and LSD give you an overwhelming urge to be in and interact with nature. Mix a little LSD into your friends' gimlets, wait until they can taste feelings, and then re-propose taking a camping trip in the woods. You may have to spend the entire weekend keeping your friends from "communing" with a big patch of poison ivy, but frankly it's better than nothing.

> **FIELD NOTES: MOST PROFOUND REVELATION ONE OF YOUR FRIENDS HAD WHILE STONED OFF HIS BALLS IN THE WILDERNESS**
>
> "Time is *cyclical*, man! That's why we can never truly die!"

Option 20.2: Bug-Bomb Them

`GASLIGHTING/MIND GAMES`

File a complaint on behalf of each of your friends to their respective landlords that all of their apartments are absolutely riddled with bed bugs. As soon as they collectively realize that they're all going to be homeless for the next couple of days while their buildings are being gassed, pulling up a Redskins camping chair around the fire and cracking open an endless stream of ice-cold Coors might not seem so bad after all.

Objective #21: Get Your Friends to Help You Move. Again.

Friends are among the most important people who'll touch our lives. They pick us up when we're down; protect us when we're in danger; and stand by our side when we feel vulnerable and alone. Unless you need help moving for the second time in three months, that is. Then suddenly they're less concerned with touching your life and more concerned with taking an embarrassingly fictional business trip to Phoenix that weekend, and all the free coffee and bagels in the world won't get them to stay. It's not your fault that that last apartment didn't work out. You know plenty of people who have found successful living situations on Craigslist and it's not *that* weird you thought "pegging" was some weird Web 2.0 verb like "tweeting" or "poking." Now you're stuck with one Saturday to move your entire life across town and you can't get a firm "yes" out of anyone to come over and lend a hand. Before you throw in the towel and either hire movers or invest in a strap-on (and it *is* an investment), manipulate your friends to help out with one of the following.

Option 21.1: Get Them All Coked Out of Their Gourds

PROJECT MK-ULTRA

If an 8-ball helped you write your senior thesis in one weekend, it should give your friends enough oomph to help you move— anything to burn off that excess energy. Just be prepared for your DVD collection to be reorganized and all the Vicodin from your tonsillectomy to be gone at the end of the day, too.

OTHER THINGS AN 8-BALL HELPED YOU ACCOMPLISH

- A four-minute mile
- A speed-reading of *The Iliad* in the original Attic Greek
- An allegorical mural of Columbus discovering the Americas on your bedroom wall
- Build a LEGO replica of Versailles
- Write the Wikipedia episode guide for *NewsRadio*

Option 21.2: Pull a Tom Sawyer

PROPAGANDA

When Tom Sawyer didn't want to paint his Aunt Polly's fence in *The Adventures of Tom Sawyer*, he tricked his friends into wanting to do it for him by telling them that it was the most fun thing since a hoop and a stick and *eff* off—it's all mine. As a nod to Mark Twain, brag to your friends about how fun moving is and how happy you are that you get to do all that packing and lifting yourself. They'll start horning in faster than they did when you won five bottles of Bacardi O at a Unitarian church raffle.

CHAPTER 3

PAVLOV'S GIRLFRIEND

SEX AND RELATIONSHIPS IN A BRAVE NEW WORLD

Nothing beats the beginning of a relationship: you can finally deactivate that JDate profile you maintain so Grandma accepts that you're *trying*; you're getting laid on a regular basis; and you have the constant nausea that only the anxiety surrounding a new love can provide. But as time wears on, you begin to realize that you're not nauseated because she called (!!!), but because she's declared tonight Adrian Zmed movie night. Again. People will tell you that compromise is the key to any successful relationship, but those people have never had to sit through *Grease 2* with an actor's commentary featuring Lorna Luft. You could ask her nicely if tomorrow night could be Paul Verhoeven night, or you could brainwash her and make *every* night Paul Verhoeven night.

Objective #22: Create a False Memory of a Romantic Getaway

There is no reason to leave Grand Forks, North Dakota. The air is clean and the people friendly. The women have a hearty beauty one can only obtain through generations of Norwegian intermarriage and a beef-rich diet. The men can fix their own cars, but always have clean fingernails. Summer brings the scent of sweetgrass rolling in off the great American prairie, while the winters are heavy with the serene, austere beauty of snow. People say "please" and "thank you" here. Gosh, they even say grace here. If you'll pardon my French, it's a helluva town. It's even got a flight school, so if you fail out of UND–Grand Forks, you can still be a crop duster and get your piece of the American dream! And yet, she still wants to go to the beach to see a "real live" jellyfish, get a henna tattoo around her ankle, and load up on risqué shot glasses. There's no need to spend hundreds of dollars to fly to Corpus Christi for the privilege of getting a sunburn and stepping on a horseshoe crab. You can make some wonderful memories without even having to leave the house! She'll thank you when she doesn't get her wallet stolen out of the toe of her Keds or food poisoning from the "beach crabs" at Cap'n Dale's Surf 'n Suds.

Option 22.1: Dude, Where's My Puka Shell Necklace?
GASLIGHTING/MIND GAMES

Challenge your girlfriend to a drinking contest, but after the first glass, refill your glass from your own private stash of O'Doul's. After she yells, "Here we go Bison, here we go! *Sioux suck!*" and collapses (you can always tell a Fargo girl—she can't hold her liquor), spring into action. Sprinkle some sand into her shoe, throw a load of towels and bathing suits in the wash, and dress her in an oversized T-shirt that reads, "F.B.I.: Federal Bikini Investigator." For extra realism, pour some mango Cruzan in her hair for that "island scent" and hold a sunlamp over her face for a few minutes for a sun-kissed look. Then spend the rest of the evening Photoshopping the two of you in an array of interchangeable beach scenes. When she wakes up the next day, remark that it's good to finally see her up and suggest that next time she not follow up her sunstroke with a piña colada chaser. (But at least you got that souvenir photo from the medical tent captioned: "I got expert medical attention at Port Aransas!" As long as you're Photoshopping, you might as well have a little fun.)

COERCIVE PERSUASION: OTHER GOVERNMENT AGENCIES SKEWERED BY RACY T-SHIRTS

- C.I.A.: Cunnilingus If Asked
- N.S.A.: Nice Sexy Ass
- D.O.D.: Drunk on Dick
- H.H.S.: Hot and Horny Services
- H.U.A.C.: Hung, Unemployed and Cheap

Option 22.2: We're Gonna Need a Bigger Boat

SUBLIMINAL MESSAGES/HYPNOSIS

Record the messiest, most disturbing specials from *Shark Week* and play them while she sleeps. After a few weeks, she won't be able to look at a body of water larger than the bathtub without hearing the slow "baaaaaaadump . . ." of the *Jaws* theme. After a few more weeks, you'll need a marine biologist and a priest just to get her to go tubing in the Red River of the North again.

Objective #23: Get Your Friend to Experiment with You Sexually

Your first semester at Bryn Mawr has really opened your eyes to how society confines us in rigid gender and sexuality categories. You want to reject the notion of a gender binary and become a more sex-positive, cisgendered, polyamorous pansexual, but sometimes the journey of a thousand miles begins with a single step. And that step is to lez out with one of your friends. You think you're ready. You spent all weekend taking notes on the first season of *The L Word* and acting out "dyke drama" (like straight drama, but louder and a lot more frequent) between two gender-queer sock puppets you made out of an old pair of thigh highs. You pierced your tongue and went through your dorm room with a fine-tooth comb to make sure you hadn't gendered the space. (You hadn't.) Now all that's left to do is to convince one of your friends to explore this exciting new sexual terrain with you.

Option 23.1: Everyone's Doing It!

PROPAGANDA

Convince her to stay in with you one night and watch a double feature of John Cameron Mitchell's polyamorous comedy-drama (yes, that is a genre) *Shortbus* and the 1979 classic *Hair*. Hopefully the feisty, free-love antics depicted in these movies will be enough to get her engine running and her juices flowing.

Option 23.2: Get Her Drunk

PROJECT MK-ULTRA

If there's anything you've learned from twelve years of all-girls Catholic schooling, it's that when girls are bored, alone, and under the influence of a few Mike's Hard Lemonades, they do more experimenting than Marie Curie trying to find polonium. When boys are around they do it for attention, and when they're alone they do it for practice. Right now, either will suffice.

Option 23.3: Tape Scissors All Over Your Walls and Hope She Gets the Hint

SUBLIMINAL MESSAGES/HYPNOSIS

If she doesn't get that you want to scissor with her, just say it's an instillation art piece and apologize to your RA for ruining the paint job when you rip the tape off at the end of the year.

OTHER THINGS YOU NEED TO APOLOGIZE TO YOUR RA FOR AT THE END OF THE YEAR

- Laughing in her face when she invited you over to watch the Oscars and drink mocktails
- The whiskey and V-8 vomit stains—that was a *night*
- That time she needed to study but you just really needed to blast some Ani
- Having diarrhea in the shared bathroom and blaming it on the janitor
- Stealing a couch from your lounge, putting it in your dorm room, and then experimenting sexually with your roommate on it

Objective #24: Get Your Partner to Be More Sexually Adventurous

Why did you and your girlfriend go to all the trouble of establishing a safe word if you're never even going to use it? It's like that $500 climbing apparatus you bought your cat that just sits there and collects dust while she has the time of her life jumping in and out of an empty Nordstrom bag. It silently mocks you for its corner of the basement as if to say, "Bless your heart—you actually thought I'd get used!" It's not like you want to do anything *that* depraved in bed. In a world where Japanese businessmen pay professional dominatrices to swaddle them in latex and bottle-feed them lunch between 401(k) meetings, wanting to slip it in your girlfriend's butt on New Year's Eve seems almost prudish by comparison. And yet every year when the ball drops, there you are, chipping away at the same block of marble you were last year, like a sculptor with an elaborate vision and a short attention span. If you've decided that this is the year you two are finally going to step out of your sexual comfort zones, get your partner moving with one of the following.

Option 24.1: Hypnotize Them with Anal Beads

SUBLIMINAL MESSAGES/HYPNOSIS

Okay, okay, okay—your partner doesn't have to try them if they don't want to. But there's nothing stopping you from taking the long string of beads out of its package, dangling it in front of your partner's face, and slowly swinging it from side to side. Once your partner is lulled into a hypnotic state, perhaps gently *suggest* that when they wake up, they return to the bedroom with a mind as open and accepting as their beautiful heart. And maybe choke you sometime.

BACKUP PLAN: IF THE ANAL BEADS DIDN'T WORK

- A riding crop
- A nipple tassel
- Anything that visually vibrates
- The noose you use for autoerotic asphyxiation
- A gigantic dildo (hell, it's eye-catching)

Option 24.2: Treat Them to a "Real Sex" Marathon

PROPAGANDA

Nothing shifts your sense of what's sexually "normal" like HBO's popular documentary series, *Real Sex*. Each hour-long episode explores popular sex fads from the bizarre (foot fetishes) to the *supremely* bizarre ("Pony Play"). The most disturbing part of the show, however, is that while the people featured on it are some of the most sexually adventurous in the country, they also look like they could serve you chicken-fried steak at your local Waffle House and tell you to have a "blessed day" before leaving the check. Once your partner realizes that even kind Mrs. Johnson across the street enjoys a good old-fashioned rim job every now and then, they'll reconsider the definition of a "crass" request.

Objective #25: Get Your Significant Other to Join You in a "Lame" Activity

When two people spend an entire lifetime together, it's only healthy for them to pursue individual activities and interests. That said, Ren Fest is very important to you. Maybe it's the enchantment of a bygone era; maybe it's the warm, accepting nature of the Ren Fest community; or maybe it's the five-dollar "bottomless horn" of mead in your hand. But standing there in the middle of the Delaware State Fairgrounds drunk in a codpiece is simply where you feel most like *you*. Up until this point, your significant other has accepted your yearly jaunt to 1507, but she hasn't fully embraced it. In short, she treats your love of Ren Fest like a retired marine colonel treats his son's homosexuality: it's tolerated as long as it's not mentioned at the dinner table. This year, however, you especially want her to be there since the King's grace has seen fit to elevate you to the title of Duke of Redhook. (Or, an honor you won in a raffle last year.) Whereas in 1507 this news would have been cause for celebration, today, her only reaction was, "Up to ye old Dumbassery again, I see." Get her in the festive spirit with one of the following strategies.

Option 25.1: Seek Professional Help

GASLIGHTING/MIND GAMES

Convince your significant other to "explore" the issue in couple's counseling. Before your first session, bribe the doctor to agree with you and tell your partner that she's not being supportive of you during this important writ of passage. She should realize that sometimes love means standing in the middle of a field in a corset feeling like an asshole.

Option 25.2: Kidnap Them and Force Them to Participate

ABUSE/TORTURE

This strategy should only be used in an extreme circumstance, when there is literally no other option. Kidnapping another human being—even if she's your wife—is illegal, morally bankrupt, and a gross violation of trust and personal freedom. But thank God it's 1507 and if she protests, it's the ducking stool for her!

FACT SHEET: REASONS WHY REN FEST IS AWESOME AND YOUR WIFE IS A DUNCE

- Units of measurement like "flagon" and "hogshead"
- If it's not fried and on a stick, it's not food
- Heaving bosoms by the fistful
- Whimsical hair braiding
- Loser goth kids acting sexually liberated, in an ugly way
- *Pewter, Pewter, Pewter!*

Objective #26: Get Your Boyfriend to Quit His Terrible Band

Most of the time, it seems like you and Bryce were made for each other. You both love going on long hikes, spending hours and hours at all-you-can-eat buffets, and the turgid, pedantic novels of John Updike. It would be a match made in heaven, if only Bryce weren't so attached to his God-awful post-punk/ska "project," Wishin' Ain't Gettin' and the Zig-a-Zag-Zooms. They don't seem to have written any songs; their practices all seem to be an hour of tuning, two hours of generalized jam session, and then two more hours of getting drunk and watching porn with the volume low enough that they think you can't hear it. It's good for him to have a project, but you can't face the thought of spending another Thursday night hearing a mediocre trumpet player trying to get through a Grateful Dead guitar riff on the brass instrument. Pull a Yoko and get your boy out of the band.

Option 26.1: Beethoven Syndrome
GASLIGHTING/MIND GAMES

Convince your boyfriend he's going deaf and has no choice but to quit the band. Each night as he sleeps, place one drop of liquid candle wax in each of his ears and let it flow down the canal. Soon, he'll realize his hearing isn't as acute as it was even recently, and he'll tearfully leave the band amid protestations that "it has to be about the music, it *has* to," and promises that he will never forget his bros, ever.

Option 26.2: Destroy from Within
DESTABILIZATION

One of the many, many things bands often break up over is women. Cheat on your boyfriend with another member of the band in such a way that it will soon become common knowledge. When your boyfriend confronts you about it, tearfully say that you're sorry, it's just that it always seemed like you weren't dating him, you were dating the band, and that ultimately you cheated on him with another band member to feel close to him. This is all a crock of shit, of course, but people in bands love to think that they're being really intense about it, so he'll probably swallow the whole story. It won't take much luck for the resulting tension to pull the band apart forever.

PERSONNEL: MEMBERS OF THE BAND YOU COULD CHEAT WITH

- Todd (bass): He has sixteen different bongs, but only one T-shirt
- Kyle (trumpet): He's not bad-looking, but he has that weird lip callous people who play wind instruments get
- Clarissa (drums): Probably not a lesbian, but you might be able to convince her it would be striking a feminist blow against the male-dominated music industry
- Hal (saving up for a keyboard): You've never been able to tell if Hal has Asperger's or is just an asshole, and you don't really care

Objective #27: Get Rid of Your Husband's Tacky Mistress

Except for a brief moment during the actual ceremony, you and Hubert never pretended to marry for love. Your family owned a sugar plantation and his family owned a rum distillery, and if you married each other the operations could combine and you would both be obscenely rich. After the "I do" and the resulting absurd wealth, you've mostly led individual lives, getting together occasionally to be seen at board meetings and the odd Memorial Day key party down at the country club. This businesslike arrangement suited you both perfectly well until a few months ago, when your husband got a new mistress named Earlette. Earlette had been stripping at "Udders n' Rudders," a nautically themed titty bar down by the marina, when in walked Hubert and a love was born. Ever since she became involved with Hubert, she's been running around town like a wild animal, going into boutiques and yelling, "I want some classy shit! I bagged a rich one so I want something real high-class and sparkly that shows a lot of boob." Ordinarily you'd just let it pass, but you and Hubert share a joint country club membership, and if he gets kicked out for letting Earlette stomp across the golf course in six-inch divot-producing stilettos, you'll be right behind him. Time for class warfare.

Option 27.1: Remove the Sticking Point
PROJECT MK-ULTRA

Next time you and Hubert are having a quiet drink together, wait until his attention is diverted, then add a moderate amount of mercury to his cocktail. You don't want to kill him, just interfere with the plumbing a little. When Earlette discovers that her new provider can't provide certain physical activities anymore, she'll scoop the hotel Gideon Bible into her purse and be out the door before he can say "This has never happened to me before."

Option 27.2: Family Ties
DESTABILIZATION

How many Earlettes can there be? Track down her family, call them up, and let them know exactly what she's doing—feel free to add a little embellishment about "breaking up your home." Before long, one of her relatives will have scolded her so fiercely that she'll feel guilty enough to break it off with Hubert.

BEHAVIOR PATTERNS: OTHER THINGS EARLETTE DID WHILE A GUEST AT THE COUNTRY CLUB

- Soaked her feet in the punch bowl
- Filled her purse with little bottles of lotion from the ladies' room
- Pronounced "shrimps" as "scramps" and ate them by the fistful
- Used dental floss at the table
- Interrupted a piano recital to sing an off-key bump-and-grind rendition of "Hey, Big Spender"

Objective #28: Get a Divorce

It's not that you have anything against Edna; it's just that, at this point, you don't really have anything *for* her, either. You got married in a hurry in front of a justice of the peace because she thought she was pregnant; the "baby" turned out to be an intense case of gas and bloating following a "power hour" at a nearby Indian buffet. Since all you really had in common to begin with was a lonely Thursday night at the pool hall and an infant that turned out not to exist, you assumed that you and Edna would gracefully part ways. Alas, no. Edna has announced that she was raised "the old-fashioned way," which apparently means that she can go home with strange men from the pool hall whenever the mood strikes her, but if she accidentally marries one due to complications from a partially fermented batch of curry dai lal, she has to try to make the marriage work. That's all very well for her, but you simply can't face a life of Tuna Helper skillet meals and crocheted protectors for the couch arms. Convince Edna it's best to part ways.

Option 28.1: The Obvious

`ABUSE/TORTURE`

Show her how terrible married life can be. Introduce a new arm-chair sport called "pin the beer can on the wife," which is played by throwing your empties at her. Miss the toilet about half the time. Wake her up six times a night by blaring Iron Maiden an inch from her ear. Her tune will quickly change from "Stand by Your Man" to "50 Ways to Leave Your Lover."

Option 28.2: A Lot of Lifetime Movies

`LUDOVICO TECHNIQUE`

Double-dog-dare her to sit through the Lifetime Movie Channel Very Special Event, *Free at Last: A Day of Divorce Dramas.* By the time she's seen TV icons Jean Smart, Annie Potts, Meredith Baxter Birney, Shannen Doherty, and Phylicia Rashad ditch their husbands and strike out as empowered single women, she'll come to think filing for divorce is the latest cool thing for a woman to do.

AUDIO-VISUAL AIDS: THE "ON MY OWN" MONTAGE THAT EVERY MOVIE ABOUT DIVORCE HAS

In every Lifetime movie about divorce or separation, there's always a cheery little montage in which the female protagonist makes positive changes in her life. Generally, she gets a haircut, buys some stylish new clothes, signs up for a pottery class, starts exercising, goes out on the town with some old friends, and, in the final shot, repaints a room in her home and then leans forward on the roller, smiling with the satisfaction of a job well done.

Objective #29: Convince Your New Husband You're a Virgin

Ultimately, it boils down to a feminist issue. If a man were successful but lonely and got a mail-order bride from some ex-Soviet republic's surplus-women fire sale, people might snicker, but no one would scold him. Yet you, a successful but lonely woman, registered an account at MyAlbanianHusband.biz, and suddenly everyone's up in your grill, giving you condescending advice about "valuing yourself more" and "thinking before you act." They can huff and puff all they want: you've made your choice, and you feel confident about it. Gjokë is a twenty-eight-year-old electrical engineer with a neatly groomed mustache and reasonable expectations. He enjoys cooking, taking long walks through the countryside, and reciting traditional Albanian ballads; you like cooking and walking and can probably arrange to be at the beauty shop during the ballads. Unfortunately, it wasn't until Gjokë was on the plane to America that you read the fine print on the website. Apparently Albanian men expect to marry virgins, and if he finds that, shall we say, *the seal has been tampered with*, he's very likely to turn on his heel and go directly back home. Make sure you get off to a good start with your Adriatic heartthrob by letting him think he's the first.

Option 29.1: What a Party!

PROJECT MK-ULTRA

Insist on observing a traditional Albanian wedding, complete with dowry, celebratory gunfire, and the consumption of massive amounts of raki, the Albanian version of the pan-Mediterranean anise liqueur. Raki is white and strongly flavored, so Gjokë won't notice if you slip a handful of crushed Xanax into one of his final glasses of the night. He'll go down like a prizefighter at the end of a nine-round beating. The next morning, when he revives, thank him for being so gentle with you and mention that the sheets are already in the wash.

Option 29.2: Fake-Out
GASLIGHTING/MIND GAMES

There's no graceful way to say this. Hide a ketchup packet in your garter, insist on wearing it to bed, and stealthily squirt a blot of ketchup on the sheets at some convenient point during the night. Again, you should probably try to get the sheets in the wash sooner rather than later, or the ketchup might attract ants and blow your cover.

LIST OF TERMS: OTHER LABORED EUPHEMISMS FOR NOT BEING A VIRGIN

- "The lottery ticket has already been scratched."
- "The dots have been connected."
- "The hall pass has already been initialed."
- "The action figure has been removed from its original packaging."
- "The colony has been opened to settlers."

Objective #30: Get Your Wife to Put More Effort Into Her Appearance

Marriage has brought you more happiness than you ever dreamed possible. You didn't think you could ever be so reassured during a difficult day at work, just by knowing that Cynthia would be there when you got home, and that she will be genuinely interested in the answer when she asks how your day was. From the smell of her famed Stroganoff Surprise simmering on the stove to the daffodils she planted along the front walkway, she adds all the little touches that make your house a home. In all your years together, you've only found one thing about Cynthia to complain about: As the years go by, she looks more and more like a cartoon mother-in-law. The first time you saw her come downstairs in a ratty, pink terrycloth bathrobe with curlers in her hair, a green herbal masque on her face, and a cigar clamped in her teeth, you thought she was kidding. But now, that's just what you expect when you get home. You don't want to hurt her feelings by telling her she looks like she's a rolling pin away from an "Old Battle Axe" Halloween costume. Get her to pretty up without hurting her feelings with one of these tricks.

Option 30.1: You May Already Be a Winner

GASLIGHTING/MIND GAMES

Cynthia will surely take the time to fix herself up if she thinks she's constantly on the verge of being on TV. Begin sending your wife letters that claim to be from Publisher's Clearing House, indicating that she may already be a winner. If she is, the camera crew and the guy with the oversized check will come by her house sometime in, say, the next eighteen months to two years. Keep being vague about the dates and you may be able to keep her in a state of made-up, coiffed readiness for the better part of a decade.

Option 30.2: Wives and Lovers

DESTABILIZATION

Cynthia will also be more likely to keep herself up if she fears competition. Claim that your car is acting up, requiring you to cadge rides home with some of your coworkers. These coworkers, however, will be sexy escorts you've hired for this specific purpose. After a week of seeing you pull up riding shotgun to beautiful women, she'll come to believe that your office is teeming with hot broads. The next time your wife considers greeting you at the door in curlers and masque, she'll think back to those women and put herself together before coming downstairs.

CHEMICAL ANALYSIS: HOW STROGANOFF SURPRISE DIFFERS FROM STANDARD BEEF STROGANOFF

Add a tablespoon of ranch dressing and few good shakes of cumin as the sauce is simmering.

Objective #31: Get Your Wife Over Her Baby Fever

The whole situation has become frankly unsettling. Every time your wife sees a baby on the street, on the TV, or in an ad for affordable life insurance, she stands stock still, crinkles up her face, and starts cooing. "Ohhhh! Da widdle bay-bee! Him so adorable! Yes he is! Yes he is!" The first time this happened you naturally assumed she had a case of rapid-onset schizophrenia, but the child's mother gave her a knowing smile, and you realized with horror that this was A Woman Thing. Your wife now behaves as though one of her ovaries has broken free and taken control of her brain. At least twice a week you catch her looking at herself in the mirror as she caresses the belly she's made by stuffing a throw pillow under her shirt. She's begun decorating the spare room as a nursery by sponge-painting little bluebirds all over the walls. Most ominously, she recently returned from a shopping trip with two significant items: a sexy nurse outfit and a home ovulation detector. She's ready to be fruitful and multiply, but you'd rather not just yet. You just bought a new Celica, and you have no desire to trade it in for a practical, reliable sedan a child's going to have fluid-based accidents all over. Cool your wife's reproductive frenzy before it's too late.

Option 31.1: Live Birth

LUDOVICO TECHNIQUE

YouTube is so full of half-assed acoustic guitar tutorials and illegally uploaded episodes of *Who's the Boss?* that it's easy to forget that it can also be highly educational. Make a playlist of natural births, throw in a couple of caesarians, then sit your wife down in front of the computer screen with some popcorn and a large Pepsi. She'll want to look away, but she won't be able to. By the sixth time the obstetrical nurse calls for the episiotomy scissors (yes, *scissors*), your wife will be so horrified you'll have no trouble talking her into compromising on an adult Boston terrier.

**ANIMAL BEHAVIOR: REASONS WHY ADOPTING
AN ADULT BOSTON TERRIER MAKES MORE SENSE
THAN HAVING AND RAISING A CHILD**

- If the Boston shits on the floor when it's twelve years old, you don't have to take it to a psychiatrist.

- You can just have the Boston spayed and not have to deal with its hormones.

- You'll never have to tactfully ask the Boston terrier if it would like you to make it an appointment with a dermatologist.

- Your Boston terrier is unlikely to bring home a pothead boyfriend named Danny "Trip" Triparelli.

- Boston terriers never threaten suicide when they get waitlisted at UC–Boulder.

Option 31.2: Field Trip

ABUSE/TORTURE

Find out when the ADHD Outreach Foundation hosts its annual outing to Chuck E. Cheese, then announce to your wife that you feel like pizza for dinner that night. As your wife watches the wired little fartlings run up and down the ramps of the skeeball games, pummel the costumed hosts, and throw up in the prize vats of the claw machines, all the while screaming and screaming and *screaming*, casually mention that you can go home and escape all this, but those poor parents . . .

CHAPTER 4

HOW TO GET A 4.0 AT SYMBIONESE STATE UNIVERSITY

MIND CONTROL AT SCHOOL

You thought Evergreen State's reputation for being an eco-anarcho-nihilist oasis in the gendered whiteocracy that is the American higher education system would translate into an open-minded approach to things like grades, attendance, and sobriety. Unfortunately, the neo-feudal fascists at the regional accreditation bureau aren't that enlightened and have instituted their oppressive norms on the Evergreen State learning community, creating an apartheid-style hierarchy where students are expected to "learn" from "teachers." In layman's terms this means that you're failing Statistics because you've shown up twice and both times you were tripping on pot falafel. You could drop out and work at a collectively owned vegan poutine stand on Whistler Blackcomb, or you can use these techniques and beat The Man at his own game.

Objective #32: Keep Your RA from Narc-ing Out

It's a typical Tuesday afternoon in March. After a huge amount of effort, you managed to go to both Introduction to Oceanography *and* Special Topics: Borges, and now you're having your "You Time." Too bad for Johnny Law that your "You Time" involves turning on *A Very Peter, Paul, and Mary Christmas*, firing up your bong ("Steinbeck"), and enjoying the grammatical zen of editing random Wikipedia articles for style and clarity. ("Mrs_Braff91" knows the title to every episode of *Scrubs* but not how to use a semicolon.) Just at the climax of "O, Holy Night," as Peter, Paul, and Mary nail the high notes in "fall on your knees!," The Man, having smelled your "Christmas cheer" down the hall, bursts into your room. The Man in this instance is Darrin, a twenty-year-old Econ major originally from Fort Collins with a cauliflower ear and a bad attitude. As he announces, "You're busted!" and fumbles for his citation book, you have but a few seconds to talk him out of it because this would be strike three for you, after your Mardi-Gras-in-November vomiting-off-the-fire-escape debacle and your aborted theft of a common-area panini press. It's time to take control of the situation.

Option 32.1: Convince Him He's Dreaming
GASLIGHTING/MIND GAMES

You're stoned and he's an idiot. You can easily do or say something strange enough to convince him he's still dreaming and if he hits the snooze button one more time, Meghan McCain might show up and do some jumping jacks. Calmly undress while mumbling in Latin, and then ask him to pass up his homework. If he asks what's going on, explain, "Oh it's been this way since the accident.

I don't make the rules, I just enforce them," and crab-walk out of the room. Hopefully you've disoriented him enough that he'll go back to his room and wait for Meghan.

Option 32.2: He Kissed Me and It Felt Like a Hit

LOVE-BOMBING

Put all your chips on green and give the wheel a spin. Take a deep hit from "Steinbeck," passionately lace your fingers through Darrin's bowl cut, and place your lips over his. As he draws in a breath to say, "What the heck are you doing?" exhale all of the smoke from your lungs into his. The suddenness of the kiss will poleax him for the minute it takes for the marijuana to take effect. And then he'll either get real paranoid or real mellow. If it's the former, he'll run back to his room and hide. If it's the latter, you might have to have a conversation with him about how time is cyclical, but it beats another talk with the dean about "choices."

BUZZWORDS: OTHER GOOD BONG NAMES

- Mary Worth
- John the Revelator
- Boomstick
- Jessica Walter
- Smaug
- Green Lightning
- Hermione Granger
- Candle in the Wind

Objective #33: Brainwash Your Way to Perfect Attendance

Remember that day in high school when you decided to "live dangerously" and skip AP Computer Science to eat Kix and watch *Andy Griffith* reruns at your buddy Steve's house, but his mom came home unexpectedly and you guys totally got busted? Remember how your dad sat you down that night and told you that next year you'll be at college where professors don't even *care* if you come to class—you either show up and pass or skip and fail? Well, thank God your father wears the hell out of a pair of Dockers, because that man has no idea what he's talking about. Professors, by and large, do care if you come to class. So much so, in fact, that it's pretty common for attendance to count for as much as 15 percent of your final grade. This may not sound like that big of a deal because how hard can it be to slide on a pair of Birkenstocks, shuffle your way across the lawn, and stare into space for an hour and fifteen minutes? But honestly? It's kind of hard. Despite the inspirational photos in Texas Tech's brochure of focused students swirling beakers and filling pipettes in racial harmony, college isn't all titration and centrifuges. Unless you want to snap like a twig mid-semester and lead a pantsless rendition of "O Captain! My Captain!" in the UPS store, you have to pad your schedule with a few fluff classes like Beginner's Golf and ANTH 296: Vampires in Southern Culture. It's important to point out, however, that registering for a class doesn't necessarily mean that you're going to go to said class. If your plan was to slack all semester, show up the day of the final and play nine holes while making a *lot* of Anne Rice references, you may have to brainwash your professor into thinking you were there all semester before that easy *A* drops down to a "Well, this is embarrassing" *B*.

Option 33.1: Hypnotize Your Professor During Office Hours

SUBLIMINAL MESSAGES/HYPNOSIS

Unless you know for sure that your professor collects antique pocket watches or mesmerizing pinwheels, show up to her office hours wearing the shiniest tie Wal-Mart sells, stand in front of her, and begin gently rocking back and forth. As your professor becomes more and more entranced by your tie's hypnotic power, take advantage of her highly suggestible state and "remind" her of your perfect attendance. While you're in there, go ahead and tell her to cluck like a chicken whenever someone says the word "bicycle," too. It was hilarious when they did it on your family's cruise to Boca Raton and you could certainly use a good laugh during finals.

HYPNOSIS TIP

It's not uncommon for repressed memories to surface while in a hypnotic state and you think hearing today's specials is an over-share. If shit with your professor starts to get real, a sudden clap or light slap on her hand should safely wake her up.

Objective #34: Avoid a Greek Tragedy

Say what you will about Greek life, but it's nothing if not consistent. It seems like every school has the same sororities: There's the fat sorority; the not-quite-fat-but-you-just-can't-seem-to-drop-that-last-ten-pounds-or-find-time-to-pluck-those-brows-huh? sorority; the slutty sorority; the sorority with the girls who are really, *really* pretty but don't quite know how to party and everyone agrees that it's a shame; the Jewish sorority; the preppy sorority; and finally, the cool sorority. There's really no better way to describe it; the girls in it are just so *cool.* They're the girls who are charming and attractive, but also have a little bit of "pill puff" going on so they're not too intimidating to talk to. The girls who are smart and get good grades but can also walk you step-by-step through how to grow pot in an attic. They're just . . . *cool.* If you've made up your mind that you're going to join a sorority, they're the one to join. Unfortunately, every other girl in your rush group is thinking the same thing and not all of you can be the chosen few. Pledge like you mean it with one of these strategies.

Option 34.1: Love-Bomb the Shit out of Them
LOVE-BOMBING

Never has love-bombing been such an appropriate method of brainwashing. This is what sororities are all about: vomiting fake praise up and down the blouses of people you hardly even know. Like that girl's shirt? *Welp*, now you do! Think "The Rachel" is an outdated hairstyle? It is. But *not on you, Sharon!* Their president's father has a house in Aspen? Time to strap two geography books to a pair of Doc Martens and hurl yourself down a mountain because you, my friend, are a skier. Yeah, it's pretty vapid and fake, but if you didn't want to be vapid or fake, you probably should have joined Hillel instead of a sorority.

Option 34.2: Rub a "Fresh Baked Cookies" Air Freshener All Over Yourself

`PROJECT MK-ULTRA`

Hell, if it works on the subconscious for trying to sell a house, why shouldn't it work for you? Plus it'll be a welcome break from all that Jovan White Musk and Aqua Net wafting around the house.

RECONNAISSANCE: COMMON SORORITY INITIATION RITUALS

- Lie in a coffin in your mother's wedding dress while humming "Sweet Caroline" until your sisters-to-be are satisfied.
- Get your "Big" a bucket of fried chicken and a six-pack of Bud Lime because it's going to be a long day, and why not?
- Be prepared to recite the full names of all of your pledge sisters and the exact dates that they lost their virginities.
- Weep. Openly and a lot.

Objective #35: Get Your Parents to Accept Your Bullshit Major

Woody Allen once famously said: "The heart wants what it wants. There's no logic to these things. You meet someone and you fall in love and that's that." While the odds are fairly high that what Mr. Allen's heart wanted was an incestuous relationship with his sort-of stepdaughter, he still had a point. "The heart wants what it wants." And much like how Mr. Allen couldn't control which page of the family photo album his heart flipped to and said, "*Yahtzee!*" you can't control what your life's passion is. And for you, it's Post-Sumerian Language Studies. You were so excited when you told your parents the big news over Thanksgiving break, but that excitement turned to disappointment when your father slammed the course catalogue down on the dinner table, opened up to a random page, and deadpanned, "Bonus round; try again." Well, yeah, maybe when compared to something pedestrian like accounting, Post-Sumerian may not seem "practical" or "useful" or "a language even used in the common era," but if you don't continue to transliterate Sumerian into a logosyllabic cuneiform, who will? Edward Hincks? Yeah, right, what is it, 1866? God. Nobody understands you. If you refuse to give up your passion, but aren't quite passionate enough to take out student loans and pay for your education yourself, it might be time to get your parent's support through more indirect means.

Option 35.1: Somehow Make Your Prospective Major Immediately Relevant

DESTABILIZATION

For example, in *Nancy Drew and the Case of the Dead Language and Unsupportive Parents*, hire a morally corrupt lawyer to transfer all of their money into a trust, the terms of which are written only in Post-Sumerian. "Well, lookie here! What ancient Mesopotamian language is *that*?" If they're serious about the vacation home, they'll get serious about your degree.

REFERENCE MATERIALS: OTHER STRANGELY APROPOS NANCY DREW MYSTERIES

- *Nancy Drew Needs to Borrow $2,000 to Have a Bitchin' Spring Break*
- *Nancy Drew Can't Come Home This Weekend Because There's a Golf Pros and Tennis Hos Party*
- *Nancy Drew Wishes You Could Love Her for Who She Is*
- *Nancy Drew Knew You Wouldn't Understand*
- *Nancy Drew Already Told You, Her Grades Were Low Because She Had Mono*

Option 35.2: Prey on Their Biggest Fears

CLASSICAL CONDITIONING

Every time your parents bring up what they wish you would major in, get pregnant. It's a two-man job and might be considered kind of drastic, but as soon as they recognize the pattern, they will *quickly* make changes.

Objective #36: Escape Plagiarism Charges

A lot of unsavory things are tolerated in college: wearing hemp necklaces and publicly kicking around a hacky sack, for one; room temperature light beer for another. Even having a three-way with two homely journalism majors can be explained as a youthful indiscretion and a pretty solid Saturday night. College is a time where you're actually encouraged to experiment, push boundaries, and make mistakes; if you haven't fucked up a few times, you're probably not doing it right. That being said, there's one mistake in college that's universally unforgivable no matter how bad your childhood was or how drunk you were when you did it: plagiarism. And yet that didn't stop you from copying and pasting the Wikipedia entry on Voltaire and turning it in as an essay so you could get to Shrimpfest on time. (Although in your defense, Shrimpfest only happens once a year.) You got busted, but before your professor reports you to the dean, maybe you can change her mind with a little manipulation.

Option 36.1: Dispose of the Evidence and Deny Everything
`GASLIGHTING/MIND GAMES`

Under cover of night, remove every book about Voltaire from the library and dispose of them in an eco-friendly way. (Because at this point, why not?) Bribe one of the computer science kids to add Voltaire to the list of blocked subjects in the university firewall. When your professor asks you why you cheated, say, "Voltaire who?" Hopefully her newfound inability to find any trace of this man will cause her to give you the "benefit of the doubt" and you can get back to enjoying your Parmesan lobster bake.

Option 36.2: Good Old-Fashioned Bribery
`PROJECT MK-ULTRA`

Bring a bag of Cajun shrimp and cheese biscuits to her office hours and encourage her to eat up. Soon she'll understand that anyone would do *anything* to get to Shrimpfest.

MANIPULATION TRICK: OTHER RESTAURANT SPECIALS THAT MAKE A GROWN WOMAN WEAK

- Olive Garden's bottomless salad
- Popeye's fried crawfish tackle box
- Bennigan's monte cristo (extinct)
- T.G.I. Friday's Jack Daniel's chicken

Objective #37: Get Your Roommate to Dump Him Already

There are over 6,000 people in the incoming Ohio State University freshman class and you're the one who has to live with the only girl still dating her high-school boyfriend. As far as freshman stereotypes go, The Girl Still Trying to Make It Work with Her High-School Boyfriend is a wolf in sheep's clothing. She's quiet, nice enough, and never wants to go out or party, so you delude yourself into thinking that maybe you've lucked out. While the rest of your newfound friends' roommates are coming home and vomiting Zelko into their printers or "sexiling" them the night before a big test, yours is curled up in bed with a carton of soy ice cream and a John Grisham novel. But then midnight rolls around and her boyfriend still hasn't called, and when he finally does, all hell breaks loose. She alternates for hours between sobbing and screaming and threatens to kill herself not twice but *thrice*. You shift your eyes around the room and quietly drop your cuticle scissors into your shower caddy and aren't really sure if that's the extent of your responsibility in this situation. It's loud.

It's awkward. And it happens every night. If your roommate isn't going to make up her mind that this relationship isn't going to work out, it's time to do it for her.

Option 37.1: Play the Ghost of White Trash Future

LUDOVICO TECHNIQUE

Duct-tape her to the bed and force her to watch hour after hour after hour of *Cops* to show her the harsh reality of what happens when you settle for the person you dated in high school. Breaking up with your first love might be scary, but beating your husband with a football phone in a meth-induced rage is *petrifying*.

Option 37.2: Start Slipping Her the Pill

PROJECT MK-ULTRA

A little known side effect of birth control pills is an ironic loss of libido. Therefore, go to your campus's health clinic and pick up two packs of birth control pills. Start secretly administering the first pack to your roommate to quash her sex drive and negate the need for a boyfriend altogether. Keep the second pack for yourself because you're in college now and we'd just feel safer knowing that you're on the pill.

**DEMOGRAPHICS: EQUALLY ANNOYING
FRESHMAN STEREOTYPES**

- The Stoner Who Nicknames Himself
- The Kid Who Didn't Drink in High School and as a Result Now Doesn't Know How to Hold His Liquor
- The Person Who Thinks When Anything Bad Happens You Should Tell the RA Because That's Their Job
- The Guy Who Doesn't Bathe Because, Dude, It's College
- The Guy Who Comes Out of the Closet So Hard It Makes a Hole in the Wall
- The Girl Who Lost Her Faith and Found Her Vagina

Objective #38: Tame Your Overly-Sexual-for-Attention Roommate

As *Animal House* taught us, college is a time to experiment with beer, sex, irresponsibility, and loud noises. It's perfectly reasonable to accept this as a reason to cut your fellow students a little slack; your roommate Amber, however, has simply taken it too far. Amber has realized that she likes attention, and she has further discovered that the most reliable way for her to get attention is to be overtly sexual, at all times, in any company. Amber has cut all of her shirts down to reveal either midriff or cleavage; she tried to alter one top to show both and wound up with an Ace bandage—which she wore anyway. Amber has not only named her vibrator Hayden, she's begun leaving it around the room. When you confront her about this, she says, "Oops! I guess I just got caught up in the moment. You know how it is." Amber cannot go to dinner, a study session, or to the corner store for cigarettes without steering the conversation toward her clitoris, whose exploits she discusses in so much detail it's practically a third roommate. At every· social gathering, Amber insists on playing "Never Have I Ever," asking the room if they've ever female ejaculated, then ostentatiously drinking half her beer and pouring the rest on her white tank top. Cool her berserk ardor with one of these tricks.

Option 38.1: Nip Her in the Bud
PROJECT MK-ULTRA

Put a thin layer of Mexico Joe's Ka-Bang-Bang-Pow Five-Alarm Drug War Habanero Hot Sauce on "Hayden." Ideally, she will learn this lesson the first time.

Option 38.2: Snap, Crackle, Pop
CLASSICAL CONDITIONING

She likes electronic appliances? Grand. Next time she launches into a one-woman reader's theatre version of "Messalina: The College Years," taze her. Sadly, the odds are good that she'll respond—after the twitching and involuntary bladder release—with some face-saving reflexive whore-speak like, "Mmm. Kinky." Taze her again until the pain penetrates the layer of sexed-out fog in her mind and she starts to associate yammering about sex with writhing on the ground drooling—and not in a good way.

COLLATERAL DAMAGE: OTHER THINGS AMBER LEAVES AROUND

- A heavily annotated copy of *The Story of O*
- Collages she's made out of Robert Mapplethorpe prints
- Used men
- Her home vajazzling kit
- A rough draft of an essay on the *Song of Songs*, titled "From Jehovah to Larry Flynt: The Divine as Pornographer"
- Fast-food wrappers, which aren't, on the face of it, sexual but do attract ants

Objective #39: Persuade Your Friends to Go on the Spring Break You Want

Spring break is a highlight of the college experience. Drinking a handle of tequila, passing out, and then having sex with whatever you wake up on top of is fun at any age, but in college it's considered "youthful exuberance" whereas later in life it's referred to as "that Jimmy Buffett goes gonzo behavior you think is still cute in a man of forty-three." It's traditional to go with friends, since nothing is more bonding than having your study buddy sway in front of you and try unsuccessfully to focus on your face while asking, "Brah. Brah. That girl I threw up on. Did you get her name, and do you think she likes me?" And yeah, no one's saying that isn't fun, but you've been to Panama City Beach for the past three years. It wouldn't kill you to mix it up a little bit and, say, go to New Orleans, where you could all soak up some culture and sample some fine dining—and where you personally could meet DemonLover69, a fellow patron of the erotic hookup website you've been corresponding with for several weeks. You tried asking politely, but that just led to "Brah. Nah. Brah. Nah. We're going to Florida." That's what they think *now*. . . .

Option 39.1: Tearful Farewell
GASLIGHTING/MIND GAMES

Stop eating, brushing your teeth, and taking care of your skin. When your friends get around to asking why you look so terrible, explain that you have . . . a condition. The doctors thought they could control it, but it seems to be progressing ever more rapidly and you may only last a few weeks. Months, at the most. It sounds silly, really, but you'd so hoped to eat some honest-to-goodness beignets before you went.

ESCAPING CONSEQUENCES: WHAT TO DO WHEN MONTHS PASS AND YOU DON'T DIE

You pretty much have three options: Claim a miracle cure and carry around a vial of Lourdes water until everyone gets tired of it; sheepishly admit that you'd misunderstood the doctors and it turns out you just had gas; or fess up and tell them what dopes they are. It's up to you.

Option 39.2: The Hard Sell
PROPAGANDA

Your friends think bro-style action only goes down in Florida? Drop the change for a copy of *Girls Gone Wild: Mardi Gras Madness: No Really, There's Tits*. Five minutes into the viewing, they'll suddenly be dddelighted to take a spin down to the Crescent City.

Objective #40: Get a Fulbright

College is almost over, and you have three options for afterwards: fight tooth and claw to get one of the six open jobs in North America; move back in with your parents and work on your novel; or find a way to stall until the economy gets better or you inherit a castle from a previously undiscovered aunt. One of the best ways to stall is to get a Fulbright scholarship, which will pay for you to go do research abroad for a year. Unfortunately, Fulbrights are very competitive, and you have a 2.15 GPA in your self-designed major, "Independent Learning (No Math)." Somehow, your double minors in "Boys" and "Keg Studies" don't seem like they'll help you here. You managed to land an interview with the Fulbright steering committee with your provocative research proposal, "I'll Go Shot for Shot with Anyone in Bulgaria and We'll Just *See* Who Walks Home, Boris," but you're going to have to really nail this meeting to get to go. You could carefully craft a series of cogent, connected arguments and write their key points on notecards, or, more realistically, you could just brainwash them. As usual.

Option 40.1: The Work Is Done for You

`ABUSE/TORTURE`

These poor Fulbright people have to spend hour after hour, day after day, listening to earnest little College Democrats event planners talk about how they plan to alleviate poverty in the world's least appetizing destinations. Is there ethno-religious strife? The answer is education. Are the only natural resources migrant laborers and guano? It's George Bush's fault. Did everyone in the country leave because it was full of cholera and leftover Soviet munitions that no one knew where to store? It's important to cooperate with regional powers, such as Pakistan. (Do-gooders always pronounce it "Paaahkistaaahn" so you know they know that's how it's pronounced.) After two days of this, don't you think they'd rather give the money to the nice girl who just wants to drink and flirt with foreigners? They'll be so tired of long-winded optimists that they'll feel love-bombed just talking to someone who doesn't give a damn. It may not advance world unity or scholarship, but it's healthy.

Option 40.2: The Way to a Steering Committee's Heart Is Through Its Collective Stomach

LOVE-BOMBING

If your interview is early in the day and you're worried that they're not yet shell-shocked enough by their daily drive down Righteous Indignation Lane, bring them some cinnamon rolls. Make sure they're gooey.

USE YOUR KNOWLEDGE: OTHER SITUATIONS IN WHICH HAVING CINNAMON ROLLS ON HAND COULDN'T HURT

- Traffic court
- A border crossing (and your car is, like, *pregnant* with a whole *litter* of Salvadorans)
- Nuclear war (the cinnamon rolls won't really help, but you'll have something to do)
- Your mother comes by to tell you she's read your new humor book and that menopause is not funny and you'd know that if you ever listened to her but of course you only listen when you want something to make fun of in your little books
- Anytime you have a case of the grumpies

Objective #41: Get an Extension on a Paper

Sometimes, you simply can't finish a paper on time. Yes, you did know when it was due weeks in advance, but let's not front like any essay has ever been written more than sixteen hours before it was due—Jonathan Swift finished writing "A Modest Proposal" in the carriage on the way to his publisher. By the time you were within that sixteen-hour window, you couldn't do your paper because your electricity had been cut off. Because you didn't pay the bill. Because you lost all your money on a string of bad bets at the local dog track, trying desperately to recoup some of the losses you incurred by betting on alleged "sure thing" Mysti Morning. This has given you a serviceable new credo—"Never bet on anything that sounds like a hair product that a stripper invented"—but unfortunately the resulting blackout has left you without ten lucid, well-argued pages about the communist subtext in *Living Single*. You could tell the truth and hope your professor is a gambling man, who will slap you heartily on the back and say, "Them's the breaks, champ. I took a bath on the Monaco Grand Prix this year. Get it to me when you can." It might work, but you should probably brainwash him just to be sure.

Option 41.1: There's a Perfectly Reasonable Explanation
GASLIGHTING/MIND GAMES

Buy time. Send him a corrupted file, labeled as your paper. When he replies that the file was illegible and needs to be resent, wait two days to respond, then send him an e-mail saying that you keep getting your e-mails to him returned as undeliverable. When he responds, wait two days, then appear confused about whether or not he did or didn't get your paper one of the "many" times you sent it. If you don't manage to put down the racing form and finish the paper while this is happening, you may not be college material.

Option 41.2: We Already Did This

`DESTABILIZATION`

Write your paper, print it, and grade it, adding notes in your professor's handwriting. (Give yourself a *B* or so. It won't help to get greedy.) When you hear from him about your late paper, indignantly burst into his office, waving your annotated essay. If your forgery is any good, you'll make him uncertain enough that he'll copy the grade into his gradebook, apologize, and later that night ask his wife if she thinks ginkgo biloba really helps memory or if the Chinese just want us to think so.

FINANCIAL ISSUES: OTHER EXPENSES YOU PRIORITIZED OVER THE ELECTRIC BILL

- Manscaping (it's subtle, but it really makes a difference)
- Yaquito, the Ecuadorian child you sponsor for just pennies a day
- Limited-edition Puma sneakers with bold diagonal stripes
- Life insurance, because who will care for them after you're gone?
- Rhinestone-encrusted doorknobs, to lend the house a little class

CHAPTER 5

GEORGE ORWELL, OBSTETRICIAN

MAKING A MARK ON YOUR CHILD'S *TABULA RASA*

A child's psyche is like the first fresh green shoot of spring, pressing forward toward the sun. A parent, if he's read this book, is like a Japanese gardener waiting with wire and shears, ready to bonsai the little tyke's mind into a series of creative shapes—as usual, the only limit is your imagination! Every birth is a new opportunity to really test nature versus nurture for yourself. Remember, brainwashing isn't "wrong" until your children are eighteen. Before that, it's *child rearing*. So start the manipulation when they're young and they'll thank you for their good upbringing. But then again, they've been trained to.

Objective #42: Make Your Children Eat Vegetables Instead of Just Sweets

You've tried everything: You've tried telling them that vegetables will make them grow up big and strong. You've tried telling them that vegetables are full of roughage, and that no one likes to be around a Constipated Constance. You've tried telling them that if they don't eat their vegetables, they'll get scurvy, the school nurse will notice, she'll call Child Protective Services, and they'll have to go to a foster home that almost definitely has a rusted-out Dodge Dart in the yard, full of old phone books and broken dreams, and who wants to go to prom with the rusty Dodge yard foster kid? Only porky goth chicks who plan the whole evening around absinthe that fails to arrive from Hungary on time, that's who, and do your kids want to spend prom at home watching *The Crow* completely sober? Do they?! Nothing works. Your children still just push the kale around the plate for half an hour then feed it to the dog. Feed your kids a balanced diet, by hook or by crook.

Option 42.1: Eating Us Out of House and Home

ABUSE/TORTURE

Burn the house down. When your children get home from school to find you surveying the damage as your wife sobs among the ashes, sigh heavily and say, "Now, it's not really your fault, I guess. We were just worried that you weren't eating enough, since you refuse to eat any vegetables, so your mother was making a giant crème brulee. Anyway, the butane torch burst and caught the drapes afire, and before we could put it out the flames spread and . . . well, here we are. I hope they don't give you vegetables at the homeless shelter." Once you get a new house, the guilt should get the squash off that plate right away.

Option 42.2: Like *Tiger Beat*, But Not

`PROPAGANDA`

Desktop publishing software allows anyone to create professional-looking documents. Create a hip new "zine" called "KidzNewz, the Newz 4 Kidz," featuring two key stories: "Gelatin is Made Out of Kittens" and "Robert Pattinson Only Dates Girls Who Eat Cauliflower."

**KEY PUBLICATIONS: OTHER CONVENIENT
ARTICLES IN KIDZNEWZ**

- "Expensive Sneakers Carry Drug-Resistant South American Cooties"
- "Obeying Your Parents: the Cool New Trend in the Twitter Generation"
- "Being Rational and Saying Things Once, Clearly, Instead of Three Times Interspersed with 'Like'—One Prom Queen's Story"

Objective #43: Encourage Them to Save It for Marriage, or At Least College

Now, part of the reason for having children is so *they* will eventually have children. A true joy of parenthood is imagining your genes enduring and spreading down through the generations, and knowing that centuries from now, your descendants may speak strange languages and worship alien gods, but they'll damn well have attached earlobes and be able to roll their tongues. It's not immortality, but it's close. However nice eventual descendants would be, though, you certainly don't want them *now*. Now that your children are older and preparing to leave home, you've been able to let them in on certain facts—specifically, the children now know that on Fridays, Mommy and Daddy like to pound a few sake bombs, watch some old episodes of *Diagnosis Murder*, have a spot of intercourse, and pass out. This ritual has saved your marriage, and the last thing you need is to have it interrupted by Waterfall Lady Gaga Hernandez, the two-month-old result of your younger daughter's post-prom moment of glory in an aging Datsun. Prevent having to raise your kids' by-blows by encouraging them to save sex until marriage, or even later.

Option 43.1: Act of God

`PROPAGANDA`

Here, the prep work is done for you. Most major religions can agree on two key points: (1) whoever is holding onto certain cities when the world ends wins, and (2) sex before marriage is wrong. You'll need to do some serious thinking about how to push your kids into religion, though. Are they more likely to follow your example, or to rebel? If they follow your example, well, get ready for some clean living, but if they're rebellious you've truly hit the jackpot. Keep knocking back Old-Fashioneds, watching R-rated "erotic thrillers," and using "motherfucker" as every part of speech, and make sure there's a Gideon Bible somewhere in the house.

Option 43.2: The Pill

`PROJECT MK-ULTRA`

Birth control pills look a lot like Tic Tacs, baby aspirin, and recreational Ambien. Scatter them liberally throughout your daughter's various jars and count on the law of averages. Not only will she be infertile, she'll be alert with bad breath, both of which turn off teenage boys. (Yeah, you could just take her to the doctor and get her a prescription, if you want to be *conventional*.)

Option 43.3: Monkey See, Monkey Do

GASLIGHTING/MIND GAMES

Children mirror their parents' behavior. No one is born knowing how to act on a date. If your children "somehow" get the idea that most dates involve filing each other's toenails and then playing with dinosaur figurines, well . . .

RECONNAISSANCE: FAMOUS VIRGINS

- Elizabeth I of England
- Mary of Nazareth
- President James Buchanan
- Most saints
- Britney Spears (briefly)

Objective #44: Get Your Child to Play a Sport So You Can Live Vicariously Through Her

People always complain that children just take, take, *take*. They're absolutely right. So you shouldn't feel guilty about wanting a little something in return, but unfortunately kids don't have a ton to offer. You can't even take their spare organs until they're eighteen. If you can't take anything tangibly useful from them, at least you can vicariously experience a little of their youth and vitality. Not that you've been planning this, but you can't help but notice that that younger one is *awfully* quick. Every time you explode out of your den with rolled up newspaper and spritz bottle in hand because one of them spelled out "eat shit" in the pebbles in your desktop Zen rock garden again, it's always the youngest one that zips out of the house, clears the hedge, and scampers down the block the fastest. She has all the makings of a track superstar. You would have run track yourself in high school, were it not for your peg leg and debilitating hay fever, but you still dream of ka-*thomp*, ka-*thomp*-ing your way across the finish line. If you can't do it, at least something you made can.

Option 44.1: Ocean, with Occasional Father

SUBLIMINAL MESSAGES/HYPNOSIS

Kids these days, always with their gadgets. If your daughter has one of the various iThings, she's probably noticed the feature that plays soothing sounds to lull the listener into a gentle sleep. Nab the iWhatever and hire an area nerd to help you add a gentle vocal overlay to the ocean sounds track:

Ksssssssssssh.

I want to run track.

Ksssssssssssh.

It's wasteful not to use all that Title IX money.

Ksssssssssssh.

It's important that I compete with my siblings for my parents' love, and running track can help me do that.

Ksssssssssssh.

Option 44.2: Fruma Sarah, Fruma Sarah!

GASLIGHTING/MIND GAMES

Remember the scene in *Fiddler on the Roof* in which Tevye claims to have been visited by a malevolent spirit in a dream, and uses this to convince his wife of a course of action? Tomorrow at three A.M., sit upright in bed and scream until everyone rushes into your bedroom to see what the matter is. After making a show of calming down and catching your breath, reveal that Esther Rolle's ghost appeared to you in a dream, and warned that, someday soon, your younger daughter will literally have to *run for her life.* Oh, if only there were some organized way that she could practice running and leaping over obstacles every day, so you could be sure she was safe.

COLLATERAL DAMAGE: OTHER THINGS ESTHER ROLLE'S GHOST HAD TO SAY

- "Use a coaster! You kids leave *rings* when you put a glass right on the wood, and that moisture warps the veneer."
- "No, those fancy prom dresses are deathtraps, they're so flammable. You're safer in a nice cheap one from Wet Seal. Those synthetics don't burn unless you're practically already on fire."
- "Quit slamming the door. I can hear it all the way in heaven."
- "Will you *please* listen to reason and take an extra year of math so you might get a scholarship to that four-year live-in bacchanal you want to go to so badly?"
- "Wear less mascara. You look like a farsighted hooker."

Objective #45: Convince Your Child to Marry Within Your Religion

Now, everyone loves diversity. Our country's greatest strength is the dazzling mosaic of cultures that form its fabric. Melting pot, global village, we have so much to teach one another, children are our future—you've heard this before, probably from a white lady wearing some form of turban. And while our sea-to-shining-sea Rainbow Coalition has made it possible to get practically any national cuisine "to go" and to learn conversational Somali over the course of three cross-town cab rides, it carries one awkward disadvantage. It's not that there's anything *wrong* with . . . You don't have anything *against* . . . We mean, no one here is racist, it's just that . . . Look. It would be *very nice* if your daughter married within your religion, okay? It doesn't have to turn into a big *thing*, it would just be *appreciated*. No one's disrespecting anyone's heritage or beliefs, but it would be a lot easier for all concerned if you and your wife didn't have to learn a lot of new holidays, especially those lunar calendar ones that shift all the time. If you're dead set against buying a copy of *Druze for Dummies* and making the best of it, head your daughter off at the pass.

Option 45.1: Instill a Fear of Unfamiliar Ceremonies
`GASLIGHTING/MIND GAMES`

You'll have to start this one early, but it's worth it. Every time another religion comes up in conversation during your daughter's childhood and adolescence, mention how you once read an article about how unpleasant that faith's traditional wedding ceremony is, especially for the wife. Let your imagination run free and come up with awful ordeals involving hot sand, chastity belts, and the evisceration of a live skink. This may sometimes strain credulity: "Episcopalians? Oh, those poor brides. They have to submerge themselves in crocodile dung to ensure fertility." But just keep the same casual, authoritative tone, and most of it will stick.

Option 45.2: Emotional Blackmail

LOVE-BOMBING

Spoil the *bejeezus* out of her. Ponies, tiaras, a special birthday greeting from the touring cast of *Wicked*, the whole nine yards. On her twenty-first birthday, as you celebrate her coming of age in one of the finest restaurants in Paris, and as she thanks you for her idyllic upbringing and asks how she can ever thank you, mention that there is one little thing she could do.

PEOPLE AND PLACES: ATTRACTIVE MEMBERS OF MAJOR RELIGIONS YOU CAN USE AS EXAMPLES

- Christians: Kristin Chenoweth, Denzel Washington
- Jews: Mila Kunis, Paul Rudd
- Muslims: Iman, Mos Def
- Hindus: Aishwarya Rai, Ritesh Deshmukh
- Buddhists: Michelle Yeoh, Orlando Bloom
- Atheists: Zac Efron, Jodie Foster

Objective #46: Get Your Child to Take the Bus to School

You conceived the child, you gave birth to it, you named it, you gave it a home, you fed it, you bought that *absurd* little corset to fix its aberrant spinal curvature; is it too much to ask that it get to school under its own power by taking the school bus? Little Tammy sure seems to think so. Every morning she takes her time and gets ready at a *leisurely* pace, despite being eight years old—how long can it take a child to put her hair in a ponytail and run a Piglet toothbrush over six permanent teeth? She proceeds to amble downstairs with the listless, aimless air of a raccoon in the early stages of rabies and take her time eating breakfast before—uh-oh!—invariably forgetting something crucial upstairs just as the bus appears. She makes it back down in time to decide not to run after the bus when it rumbles out of the cul-de-sac, then hollers, *"Mom! I missed the bus! Can you take me to school?! Mom? Mom!"* You can, but this will be the last time.

Option 46.1: Choose an "Instructive" Route
CLASSICAL CONDITIONING

Blame voodoo economics, blame the welfare state, blame the wrath of God: Whoever's fault it is, every American city has at least one terrifying neighborhood. Next time Tammy misses the bus, make sure the route you use to drive her to school passes down one of those streets where all the liquor stores have bars over broken windows and sick-looking dogs fight over Burger King wrappers in the middle of the street. As mean-eyed hookers mouth obscenities at your passing car and winos vomit so hard they fall down, Tammy may mention that Dan the bus driver never goes to school this way. You should respond that you're sorry she has to see all this, but it's the only way you know how to get to the school. "But don't worry. The middle school is in a different part of town, so you won't have to see any of this once you start sixth grade. Of course, we will have to go through Little Kashmir, which occasionally sees some unrest. We might need to get you a helmet."

COLLATERAL DAMAGE: IF YOUR DAUGHTER SEES SOME INTENSE SHIT DRIVING THROUGH CRACKBURG CROSSING OR LITTLE KASHMIR

A good parent can sometimes see opportunities where other parents see problems. If, while driving through a crime-ridden neighborhood, she should see a prostitute and a down-and-out local politician frantically coupling in an alley, explain that yes, that is how babies are made, but ideally this happens between people in a committed relationship, indoors, and without a monetary dimension. If you happen to pass by a sectarian gun battle in Little Kashmir, use the chance to start an open discussion about immigration quotas and the benefits of secular humanism.

Option 46.2: Laissez-Faire

ABUSE/TORTURE

Just let her miss school. If she misses so much she has to repeat the third grade, well, that's a lesson she'll have learned. If the truancy officer comes by, explain that your family members are Christian Scientists. No one really knows how the laws around that work, so she'll probably leave you alone.

Objective #47: Get Your Son to Study Harder

Be careful what you wish for, we guess. In the beginning, you were so relieved your son wasn't a nerd—no constantly mislaid inhalers, no taking rubber sheets to Space Camp, no "stress vomiting." By his teens, he actually seemed to like *both* sports *and* girls—what more could a father ask for? Well, a lot, actually. Apparently, when little Trey was in the bassinet and the good fairies were bestowing their blessings like in a fairy tale, it was a mistake to cut out after visits by the Sport Aptitude Fairy and the Heterosexuality Fairy. You should have waited for the Not Dumb as a Bag of Wet Sand Fairy, because Trey has a D+ grade average and got a letter from the SAT people telling him that he should try taking the test in his native language. If he doesn't start studying soon, you'll have to try to get him into a party trade school, if there is such a thing. Before you download the brochure for ITT Tech at Padre Island, try getting him to crack a book.

Option 47.1: The Poverty Cycle
GASLIGHTING/MIND GAMES

Convince your son that study and hard work are his only chances to escape the grinding, vicious poverty you're about to pretend your family is in. Only buy generic peanut butter, white bread, and baked beans for groceries. Before bringing in the mail, add "Final Notice" to any official-looking envelopes using a red-inked stamp. If you feel dramatic, allow your son to occasionally hear you weeping behind a locked door at night. Once this has all had some time to sink into his skull, sit him down and give an emotional lecture about the future and how he shouldn't repeat your mistakes. With any luck, he'll start studying his ears off.

Option 47.2: There's Always Drugs

PROJECT MK-ULTRA

Oh, Ritalin. You dissolve so easily in Trey's post-football practice sports drink. The action of the classic attention deficit disorder medication should give him an uncontrollable urge to do something productive, so dose him up and make sure his books are where he can find them easily. Otherwise, he might just clean out the garage.

> ## PEOPLE TO KNOW: OTHER FAIRIES WHO OCCASIONALLY APPEAR CRIBSIDE
>
> * The Fat but with Good Skin and a Sweet Disposition Fairy
> * The Can Belch on Command Fairy
> * The Social Anxiety Disorder Fairy
> * The Grows Up to Be a Whore with a Heart of Gold Fairy
> * The Irregular Period Fairy

Objective #48: Train Your Child Not to Bring Home Pets

This is a depressing way to start a Tuesday. No sooner had your son Carlos woken up than he went to the terrarium to say "Good morning" to his latest pet, a hermit crab named Señora Mercedes Watkins. Apparently Sra. Watkins was older than she let on, because not only was she dead but one of her claws had also fallen off. Once again, the whole family had to troop out to the yard and watch Carlos dig a tiny grave, mark it with a popsicle-stick cross, and lower the chitinous little body into the earth, as one of his sisters read a random page from *The Book of Common Prayer*. Sra. Watkins was placed in her final repose among Corporal Jeremiah Schratt, an anole with a nervous condition; Sister Mary Aloysius, a mouse that drowned herself in her water dish; and Mark Jenkins, a goldfish that succumbed to ennui. These are just the casualties from the last few weeks; if someone dug up this area they'd find enough tiny bones to make a witch doctor's summer wardrobe. It's getting depressing, and you're afraid the constant exposure to death might warp Carlos—he's already dressed in black as "mourning" for the crab. Make him realize that animals are best loved from afar.

Option 48.1: Release Swarms
`ABUSE/TORTURE`

The difference between pets and vermin can be so very, very thin. Release the occasional swarm of something in the house—tarantulas, roaches, basset hounds, what have you—and watch as Carlos's childlike love of animals turns to an adult hatred of fuss, mess, and crawlies.

Option 48.2: Based on a True Story
`LUDOVICO TECHNIQUE`

Children are so trusting. For example, many children who watch a *Pet Sematary/Pet Sematary 2* double-header will believe their parents when they say, "Oh, yeah, this is based on a true story. This one happened in Maine, but it happens all over the place. Pets come back sometimes. Usually they come back evil when they do. No one knows why, but they always want revenge for something."

**AUDIO-VISUAL AIDS: OTHER MOVIES
WHERE A KID BROUGHT HOME A PET
AND SHIT WENT DOWNHILL REAL FAST**

- *Gremlins*
- *Cujo*
- *Old Yeller*
- *National Velvet*
- *Fatal Attraction*

Option 48.3: Good Country Folk

CLASSICAL CONDITIONING

Move to a farm, where Carlos can get the benefit of fresh country air and wide-open spaces to play, and where animals either work or get eaten. He'll learn not to name the piglets after seeing exactly how bacon "happens."

Objective #49: Get Your Child Admitted to a Fancy Boarding School

You're ordinarily not much of a snob, but you'd love to get your daughter Gwendolyn into Miss Jessica Deptford's Preparatory Academy for Young People of Quality. The people at this exclusive, high-dollar prep school practically *shit* class, and that's the kind of person you want Gwendolyn around during her formative years. Ideally she'll meet some nice young man who rows and has a name like Warren Charles Victor "Boofy" Smythe-Warburton and get him to the altar somehow. Failing that, you suppose she'll probably get a good education in those ivy-covered buildings, and Miss Jessica's is certified résumé gold. Money's no obstacle—not since your successful tort action against Tidy Cat—but you'll still have to get Gwendolyn, her humble origins, and her less-than-stellar test scores past Miss Jessica's very strict selection committee. It's easy to pass your diamond in the rough off as a polished five-carat dazzler with a couple of basic mind control techniques.

Option 49.1: Duke of Earl

GASLIGHTING/MIND GAMES

Nothing makes snobs like those at Miss Jessica's sit up and take notice faster than a great big (fake) hereditary title. Legally change Gwendolyn's name to "Her Highness Gwendolyn von Habsburg, Duchess of Tyrol," and use the whole name on all correspondence with the school. (Make sure your stationery has a crest.) You're not lying per se, since that is her legal name—just make sure she doesn't say a word till she gets formally admitted, or they'll hear her strong South Jersey accent and get suspicious.

Option 49.2: Sob Story

PROPAGANDA

The only thing snobs like more than titles is briefly pretending *not* to be snobs by feigning an interest in the less fortunate. Write to Miss Jessica's not as Gwendolyn's mother, but as her social worker. Tell a long, poignant tale of Gwendolyn's sufferings—feel free to get creative, but it's important to say that she spent some time on the streets, in a refugee camp, or on a ventilator. They get a lot of dyslexic immigrants and orphaned cancer survivors, so really reach for the stars (or the gutter, as it were). If the tale you weave for Gwendolyn is one of the most depressing/inspiring they've heard during this application period, she's sure to land one of their charity slots. Just make sure you write down what you say, in case she has to give a speech at graduation about "overcoming" and the value of an education.

TURBO: IF YOU'RE REALLY DESPERATE

If you absolutely have to get Gwendolyn into Miss Jessica's, don't hesitate to combine options 1 and 2 above. Nothing touches rich people's hearts more than hearing about a rich person in trouble. By the time you finish telling the selection committee about how Gwendolyn crossed the Himalayas on foot, carrying her special-needs brother, making her own chemotherapy out of native herbs, carrying only her scepter and tiara as befits a princess, they'll be in tears.

Objective #50: Convince Your Child Not to Get Body Modifications

You've tried very hard to respect your son's whole "different drummer" approach to life. You let him and his idiot friends in that psychobilly band they have, Jubal T. Early and the Moonshine Bandit Crew, practice in the garage, and when you yell "Damn hippies!" you usually pretend that you're watching baseball and the San Francisco Giants are playing. You've even almost gotten to the point where you can look him in the face without laughing at his lime green soul patch/electric-blue muttonchops facial hair situation, because being a father means loving your children, even when you're unable to respect them. His latest idea, however, is a bridge too far: He wants to get a tattoo. Not just any tattoo: a full backpiece featuring a skeleton astride a rearing horse, waving a Stetson in one hand and firing a six-shooter with the other. You asked him if he was serious, and he said he was still thinking about merging the skeleton and the horse into a centaur, but basically he was serious, yeah. Time to wash this idea out of what little brain he has.

Option 50.1: So Totally Lame

CLASSICAL CONDITIONING

To an eighteen-year-old, only two things a parent can do are not "totally bogus": You can go away for a month and leave them in the house unsupervised, or you can die and leave them a no-strings inheritance. Any other parental action is, by definition, the antithesis of cool. Bring your wife with you, and go to the "hip" part of town. Get a tattoo across both your backs, so that the full panorama is displayed when you stand side by side, shirtless. Go to your son and show him immediately. Tattoos will never have looked so lame.

VISUAL EVIDENCE: THE TATTOO YOU AND YOUR WIFE GOT

Two anthropomorphic crocodiles in Hawaiian shirts are dancing at an outdoor tiki bar while holding pina coladas (in the actual coconut, of course). The lady crocodile can be identified by her earrings and extended eyelashes. Underneath it all, a caption in drop-shadow script reads, "Lovin', Laughin', Livin' Life."

Option 50.2: Trite and Derivative

GASLIGHTING/MIND GAMES

Find out which tattoo artist your son plans to use and suborn the artist with a bribe. When your son comes in with the drawing of his "bitchin' tat," have that tattooist say, "Are you sure? I been doin' a lot of these skeleton-on-horse ones lately. Must be a new fad." Of course your son doesn't want to follow the masses and get a *fad* tattoo. He's not a sheep! If you keep up your payments to the tattooist, you can have him say the same thing every time your son comes in with a fresh design idea, until he gives up the whole project as "not original."

Objective #51: Make Your Son Get a Summer Job

Oy. Your son, Freddy, has decided to be a nihilist. Oh, begging your pardon, it's no longer Freddy but *Friedrich*, as he reminds you every day. Apparently, a teenager needs a German name to sit in a darkened room all day reading *The Abridged Nietzsche* and *A Sartre Reader* by candlelight. You've tried to explain to him that what he's feeling at his age is probably just hormones, not actually angst at the final, utter futility of all human endeavors, and that it might help if he got a summer job or went on a date with a girl who didn't wear black lipstick. He responded by saying, "Oh, Mother. Your small-minded bourgeois provinciality is so *banal*. If you only *knew*," and then burying his head under a pillow. If he wants to be so condescending and glum, he can earn his own money to buy frozen pizza rolls and black curtains. Time for him to join the workforce.

Option 51.1: Give Him a Goal

GASLIGHTING/MIND GAMES

When you asked *Friedrich* if he'd like to get a summer job to earn some extra money, he laughed bitterly and said, "Oh, Mother. Capitalism is just a distraction from the progress of mortality." Well, fine, but what if he had a goal? Have a web-savvy friend mock up a website for the French Academy for Young Thinkers, a summer camp where teenagers who understand the pointlessness of all activities meet for intense discussions in the Paris catacombs. What do you know! The August session costs only slightly less than what he'll earn when he bags groceries for two months!

Option 51.2: Threaten His Sacred Privacy

DESTABILIZATION

When *Friedrich* comes out of his bedroom, sit him down. Explain that property taxes have risen recently, and that if he refuses to work to help offset them you'll have to rent the room next to his to a boarder. Actually, two boarders; you've been in touch with the local Latter Day Saints and they have a nice couple of young men who will be doing their mission in the area. "Supposedly they're very cheery young men, always waking up with a song, and with a good word for everybody." You can't be a nihilist and live on the same landing as a brace of singing, smiling, sunshiny Mormons. *Friedrich* will take a job mopping up child spit at the dollar store before he lets his moping space be invaded.

> ### CONTEXT: OTHER THINGS THAT, PREDICTABLY, *FRIEDRICH* CONSIDERS "BANAL"
>
> - High school
> - Doing his own laundry
> - Talking to his teacher about some tutoring for the AP Chemistry test
> - Turning down the Bauhaus album he plays on repeat
> - Polite conversation
> - Letting his room air a little
> - Running errands with his mother so they have some time to talk like they used to

Objective #52: Ensure That Your Children Will Care for You in Your Old Age

This is one of those days where it's just good to be alive. You're on your sixth chili cheese dog and, conservatively, your seventeenth beer. You're jumping up and down, hollering at the TV—you have no idea who's playing what, if anything, but you start instinctively jumping up and down and hollering at the TV around beer eleven. You drove to this party in your convertible with the top down, the wind running free across your shoulder where other chumps are tied down by those confining seatbelts. When you get home tonight, you're going to eat an entire lemon meringue pie, have some more beers, and fall asleep in the middle of the floor. And then, if you feel like it, you'll get up the next morning, have whiskey and steak for breakfast, then do it all again. Your friends, your family, and that nice worried cardiologist are all telling you to slow down and be careful—maybe take in a few substances that aren't fermented, deep-fried, or distilled. You don't have to worry, though. When your organs start blinking out like old neon signs, you'll have a place to go. You spent your children's whole lives training them to care for you when you got old, and here's how you did it.

Option 52.1: An Entailed Inheritance
GASLIGHTING/MIND GAMES

Tell your children the story of their batty great-great-aunt Jeanette, dead these thirty years. "She always liked me, you see, but she was crazy. She had this enormous fortune, hundreds of millions of dollars in gold, but she couldn't stand to leave the money to anyone she knew—thought they would kill her for it. So she left it in trust, not for me, but for my heirs. It's an impartible inheritance, sadly, so I can only leave it to one of my children. I guess it would only be fair to leave it to whichever one of you goes to all the trouble and expense of caring for me in my old age."

FROM THE ARCHIVES: WHAT YOUR WILL ACTUALLY SAYS

"So actually, I've just got about eight thousand in checking, which you kids can split. Sorry about the years of deception; I hope you can forgive me. If not, I'm dead, so no big loss.
Love,
Dad"

Option 52.2: A Parent Is a Child's First Teacher

SUBLIMINAL MESSAGES/HYPNOSIS

Slip the concept of caring for an aged parent into everything you ever teach your children: "Now I lay me down to sleep, I will care for my irascible old father in his dotage. Amen." "I pledge allegiance to the flag, and to my father, however querulous and incontinent he becomes." "*I* before *e*, except after *c*, and my wrinkled old father can come live with me." "It will never occur to them *not* to care for you."

CHAPTER 6

FREE DRUMSTICKS AND CHEAP GAS

EVERYDAY HYPNOSIS

By now, you've brainwashed your workmates, your friends, your spouse, and your children. You may think your work is done, but note: daily, you interact with scores more people on a more casual basis. Why neglect them? With a little know-how and effort, you can train every acquaintance you have to smooth the path for you. Meter maids will let your "creative parking solutions" slide, the doorman will tip *you* at Christmas, and the guy working at the bowling alley snack bar will open a fresh bag of liquid cheese to make your nachos. Read on, and find out how Svengali always got a free upgrade to first class.

Objective #53: Get a Cancelled Show Back on the Air

Becker, Soap, Newhart, Dilbert: The Animated Series, Herman's Head, Wings, JAG, Ghost Whisperer—these are just some of our favorite shows that got struck down in their prime. There's nothing more painful than when the hammer of the mighty television executive comes down and nails shut the coffin of another prime-time gem. But this time they've gone too far. They've cancelled *The Garry Shandling Mysteries*, in which Garry Shandling plays Garry Shandling, a sitcom actor who solves murders between takes. To make matters worse, they cancelled it in the middle of a very special two-part episode in which all of the evidence points to Jeremy Piven, but Shandling has his doubts. Maybe other people can go on with their day without knowing whether Piven was indeed the one who filled the jelly donuts with arsenic or if he was just a Patsy for that vicious Annie Potts, but not you. Clearly, the only option is to coerce the president of the network into re-greenlighting the best damn show pay cable has ever produced.

Option 53.1: Rig the Network President's Computer and TV to Only Play the Program in Question

PROPAGANDA

Rig the network president's computer and TV to only play *The Garry Shandling Mysteries* ad infinitum. It's always possible that he just doesn't know what an incendiary piece of television programming he's just cancelled. You were skeptical too, but The Shand is a born sleuth. By the time the pres becomes emotionally invested in the plot, he'll be just as devastated as you were that Piven's fate is unresolved.

Option 53.2: Bring the Show to Life and Give Him a Walk-On Role

GASLIGHTING/MIND GAMES

Some people just get more invested in live performances. Get the actors on your side and do a little guerrilla theater. For example, with *The Garry Shandling Mysteries*, stage a murder by means of a wacky weapon in the network president's office and volunteer to call the police. As luck would have it, the LAPD happened to dispatch Special Deputy Garry Shandling to the scene of the crime! He solves the murder in nothing flat with his trademark brand of self-deprecation and passive-aggressive brilliance, saving the day. Renewing the show will be the *least* the president can do to repay Special Deputy Shandling.

FACE RECOGNITION: PEOPLE WHO HAVE PLAYED THE MURDERER ON *THE GARRY SHANDLING MYSTERIES*

- Katherine Helmond
- Paul Simon
- David Spade
- LeVar Burton
- Rosie Perez
- Jonathan Taylor Thomas
- Jeff Stryker

Objective #54: Convince Your Mom That You Don't Have a Drinking Problem

Sure, you have a few glasses of Kendall-Jackson chardonnay when you get home from work to unwind, but who doesn't? And yeah, July is "Daiquiri Month" in your home, but it's summer! And there was that one time you drank an entire jeroboam of Jacquart and endorsed Dwayne "The Rock" Johnson as the compassionate conservative choice for President 2004 on your LiveJournal, but that was *college*. You enjoy alcohol, sure, but it's not a problem. Floods in Bangladesh are a problem. AIDS in Africa is a problem. But your drinking? That's just an adorable little eccentricity of yours, like dyslexia! And yet, every time you're out to dinner with the family and you casually order, "Boilermakers: line 'em up!" your mother purses her lips and gives you a little sniff. Your family trip to Napa Valley was rerouted to Knott's Berry Farm because as she told her travel agent, "We don't want to encourage her." Before the champagne toast at your cousin's wedding, she took the flute away from you, squeezed your hand, and whispered, "You're stronger than this," in your ear. You try laughing it off and reassuring her that she's being ridiculous, but that only ends in her screaming, "I don't know why my caring about you is so funny!" before she storms out of the house to do some therapy gardening. Derby Day is coming up and if you don't want to be served a "mock julep," brainwash her into thinking that if you're not sober as a judge, at least you're not drunk as a senator.

Option 54.1: Turn Her Into a Raging Alcoholic

PROJECT MK-ULTRA

Start with rum cake and work your way up. Spike her foods with beverages containing more and more alcohol until she's drinking greyhounds out of a Mason jar while screaming racial epithets at the contestants on *Wheel of Fortune*. It may seem harsh, but then again she made you take oboe lessons for ten years.

Option 54.2: Fake a Pro-Alcohol News Article

PROPAGANDA

Get to this month's *Prevention* magazine before she does and carefully insert a doctored article explaining that an alcohol intake of four or more drinks a day "energizes the womb" and leads to increased fertility, and rely on her desire for grandkids to keep the Tom Collins's coming.

PROSPECTIVE TITLES FOR YOUR PRO-ALCOHOL ARTICLE

- "Alcohol Plays Greater Role in Conception Than the Obvious, Study Finds"
- "Estrogen, Tequila Key to Uterine Health"
- "Ovaries Most Functional When Swimming in Gin Like Cocktail Olives, Scientists Say"

Option 54.3: Become an Affectionate Drunk
`LOVE-BOMBING`

Every time you've had a few, hold her in your arms, weep gently, and tell her how much you care. With any luck it'll touch her heart and she'll leave your liver alone.

Objective #55: Get Paroled

The odds are in your favor that you'll never actually be in a situation where you have to convince a panel of people to curtail your prison sentence and release you early on parole. But then again, nobody ever toddles up to Mother after a rousing career day at school, pulls on the hem of her housedress, and says, "Mommy, when I grow up, I want to work in a dying medium like terrestrial radio, drown in over $80,000 worth of student loans that I can't afford to make payments on anymore, get caught embezzling money from the WCTN fifth annual Monster Mash fund, and go to a white collar federal penitentiary in Otisville, New York, for two to five years!" Or at least you didn't. And yet, here you are: two days away from your parole hearing and only *$76,451* in the hole. (Thank God for small favors.) While you've tried to keep the shiving to a minimum and are the best mezzo-soprano the Otisville Correctional Facility's gospel choir has ever had, play it safe and brainwash the parole board into releasing you early with one of the techniques below.

Option 55.1: Win the Parole Board Over with Handmade Gifts
`LOVE-BOMBING`

You've discovered a creative fire deep within these past twenty-eight months in the clink that you never knew existed. According to your art therapist, you produced some really "powerful" work in the collage unit, and the Latin Kings and Aryan Nation know not to fuck with you because you weaved the shit out of a boondoggle keychain on your first day in the yard. Instead of selling everything you make on your Etsy website shop, win over the parole board by giving them a few of your best collages and key chains as thoughtful gifts.

FIELD NOTES: WHY THE OTHER GANGS LEAVE YOU ALONE

- Crips: You helped the leader of the local chapter file his taxes
- Bloods: You bitched up and they were impressed with your "can-do" attitude
- The Crazy Azians: You were *always* up for being a fourth in mahjong
- The Zetas: You were unfailingly polite to them, and sometimes that counts

---

Option 55.2: Get the Parole Board Drunk on Toilet Wine Before Your Hearing

PROJECT MK-ULTRA

This year's Riesling came out perfectly—flowery and aromatic with just a whisper of catsup and moldy Wonder bread. Pairs well with whitefish, pork, and an early release. Drink up.

Objective #56: Get Upgraded to First Class

Three types of people fly first class: honeymooners, businessmen, and emotionally fragile rich girls being flown home for a semester of R and R after their post-exam "suicide attempt" with a bottle of Children's Motrin. Considering you're a professional barista with a family who could only afford to send you a cookie cake after your post-exam suicide attempt, you're probably not going to find yourself on the glamorous side of the blue dividing curtain any-time soon. But oh, how you long for the comforts of first class—cashmere blankets, bottomless mimosas, and seats that actually accommodate you to spread your legs slightly so you don't get a yeast infection every time you fly home. If you can't handle one more flight in coach with the Untouchables, bump yourself up to Brahmin with brainwashing.

Option 56.1: Actually Tip Your Flight Attendants

LOVE-BOMBING

Did you know it's proper travel etiquette to tip your flight atten-dants? Like, *cash* money? And here you thought they saw you off at the end of every flight and told you to have a nice day because they actually cared, not because they expected you to slip them a little something extra for throwing peanuts at you and offering a nagging, "Sir. *Sir*. That's not going to fit, sir." That being said, if you overachieve and tip them before takeoff, they might be so flabber-gasted they'll bump you up to first class in return.

Option 56.2: Take the Kevin Smith Approach

PROJECT MK-ULTRA

Say what you will about the morbidly obese, but they have the freak's in-born sense of entitlement. Gain a shit-ton of weight until you physically can't fit into a seat in coach. When you get on your flight, make a huge scene and demand that they bump you up to a spacious first-class seat, or you'll sue them for physical disability discrimination.

MORE STUFF FAT PEOPLE DON'T HAVE TIME FOR

- One-trip salad bars
- Non-muumuu garments
- Incorrect fast-food orders (especially failure to super-size)
- Their pancreases' desperate pleas for mercy
- Pilates

Option 56.3: Tell Them You've Got the Shakes. The Hippy, Hippy Shakes.

GASLIGHTING/MIND GAMES

Tell the flight attendants that you've come straight from your alcohol intervention, you're on your way to rehab, and you need to be bumped up to first class for the champagne service or else you'll go into withdrawal on the plane and violently vomit everywhere. There's a fairly good chance that they'll see right through your bullshit, but then again, when vomit's involved, why would they risk it?

Objective #57: Have Your House Appraised for Well Over Fair Market Price

You don't want to put your home up for collateral, but it's the only major asset you have, and you really want this small business loan. (You can't believe no one has ever set up an erotic notary service before, and you believe you've found an underserved niche.) You're proud of your house, but you fear it might be undervalued at the appraisal. There's a little termite damage; the crown molding seems a little dated, now that you look at it critically; and you've never bothered to fix the hole in the wall where you threw a decorative wall sconce and narrowly missed your ex-husband Irving. You thought it added character and history, but you can see now how someone might think it looked tacky. If you really need the house to be appraised well so you can get the loan you need and follow your dream, use one of these tips.

Option 57.1: Invent a Colorful History

GASLIGHTING/MIND GAMES

Even if the house looks like a hot sack of crap, it's still valuable if it's historically important. Spin the appraiser a lurid tale of Indian raids, lost golden treasure, good-hearted whores, and how, despite being in central Michigan, the house was the capitol of the Confederacy for several desperately confused hours in 1865. Feel absolutely free to weave in a few ghosts—a good, solid haunting never fails to jack up the value. "They say, on cold nights, you can still hear Jefferson Davis saying, 'I don't think you even know where we *are*, Alexander. We've been on the road for seventeen hours. I think we're in Canada. I'm going to ask at that house.'"

SUPERNATURAL INVESTIGATION: OTHER THINGS JEFFERSON DAVIS'S GHOST HAS SAID IN HIS HAUNTING

- "Shit, that jackass Nicolas Cage is playing me in a miniseries! Why the hell didn't they get Richard Gere?"

- "Don't tell Lee's ghost this, but I've been following the Detroit Red Wings the last few seasons and I've really enjoyed it. I'm not happy about their draft picks, though."

- "Some years I float over to the Michigan Womyn's Music Festival. Those ladies are angry about a lot, but they know good music. I'm curious to see how they resolve the trans issue."

- "No, integration was a lot easier in the spirit realm, largely because we're all a uniform faded gray. Also we're all dead, so it's not like anyone uses the drinking fountains."

Option 57.2: The Heebie-Jeebies

`ABUSE/TORTURE`

Lock the appraiser in the spare bedroom with Irving's old ventriloquist's dummy, the one whose eyes seem to follow you wherever you go. After a few hours, she'll be creeped out enough to sign anything you slide under the door.

Objective #58: Convince Your Role-Playing Game Group to Let You Lead a Game

You never thought of yourself as someone who would enjoy tabletop role-playing games, but you gave it a shot a few months ago and came away a fan. Now, every Thursday finds you holed up with the guys in one of your dining rooms, slaying dragons, rescuing princesses, and giving the lusty serving wench at the alehouse hearty slaps on her fine, meaty rump. A good time is generally had by all (except for the dragons, natch) but recently you've been feeling a little discontent. Everyone else has gotten a chance to lead a game except you. You've asked, but the other guys keep saying you're "too inexperienced" or "too likely to make the whole thing a blandly instructive, almost Brechtian allegory about the arbitrary distribution and exploitation of power." You've tried sulking, pleading, and cajoling, but nothing has worked so far. Time to try manipulation.

Option 58.1: Get Them Where It Hurts

`ABUSE/TORTURE`

A role-playing game session is simply not complete without the traditional drink: buckets and buckets of that famed caffeinated nectar, Mountain Dew. Next time it's your turn to host, serve the traditional vat of Mountain Dew, but lock the doors to all the bathrooms in your house. You should probably also lock the exterior doors, to deprive them the use of a life-saving shrub. As their bladders fill and the caffeine stimulates their voiding muscles, they will grow increasingly desperate—use this leverage to extract a promise that it's your turn to lead next week.

Option 58.2: Maximum Overdrive

`PROJECT MK-ULTRA`

Long-haul truckers use concentrated caffeine pills to keep themselves awake on long nights driving across the long, unchanging miles of the Great Plains. Grind a few of these pills up and add them to the group supply of Mountain Dew. Explain that you can't have any tonight because you're trying to lose a little weight before summer bathing suit season. The thundering rivers of caffeine will beat away at their brains, and they'll spend the whole game twitching, grinding their teeth, and completely unable to focus on the task at hand. Use this as an example of why you'd be a good leader; everyone else was distracted, but you remained attentive to the task at hand.

CULTURAL STUDIES: OTHER WAYS TRUCKERS STAY AWAKE WHEN CROSSING THE EERILY EMPTY GREAT PLAINS AT NIGHT

- Picking up a garrulous hooker at a truck stop who tells her life story all the way across Nebraska, with character voices
- Singing along to a Smash Mouth mix CD at the top of their lungs
- Debating the merits of multiparty democracy over the CB
- Driving along on the rumble strip and pretending it's a theme park ride
- Mentally plotting the espionage thrillers they plan to write one of these days

---

Objective #59: Get Cast in an Amateur Theatrical Production

You've always loved attracting attention, causing a scene, and making dramatic entrances, even in the womb: Your mother went into labor with you right as Neil Armstrong set foot on the moon.

As time passed, you threw yourself into any activity that might put all eyes on you: ballet lessons, child beauty pageants, even a brief phase of starting small fires in empty buildings. You've calmed down a little since then, but you still crave the spotlight, so you were thrilled to see that your town community center was going to begin hosting shows, beginning with the classic musical about alcoholism and irresponsible parenting, *Mame*. You'd love a shot at the title role, but you'll happily settle for the boozy sidekick, the pregnant-out-of-wedlock secretary, or even Featured Party Guest. What you will *not* do is happily paint props while pretending it's so much fun just to be involved, even backstage, as you did when you were passed over in casting for the junior college production of *Joseph and the Amazing Technicolor Dreamcoat*. You're getting your time on stage, whatever it takes.

Option 59.1: Casting Couch
LOVE-BOMBING

Just sleep with the director already. Yes, it's a cliché, but the reason it's a cliché is because it works.

Option 59.2: Just Right for the Part
SUBLIMINAL MESSAGES/HYPNOSIS

Once the director is asleep, sneak into his yard, get right under his bedroom window, and sing the entire score—quietly enough not to wake him, but loudly enough to register in his subconscious. Later, at the audition, don't be surprised if he tells you that you sound exactly as he imagined the role.

Option 59.3: Beat the Hell Out of Him

`ABUSE/TORTURE`

Pop on a pair of brass knuckles, kick open his front door, think back to the time your mother told you, "You have a lot of ambitions for such a plain little girl," and give that director a savage beating. Theatre people being what they are, he's less likely to call the police than to say, "Perfect! That's exactly the kind of bitchy, queen-bee personality I need in a Vera Charles!"

MAKING COMPARISONS: OTHER ROLES YOU BRING TO LIFE WITH YOUR BITCHY, QUEEN-BEE PERSONALITY

- Rizzo from *Grease*
- The Baroness from *The Sound of Music*
- Velma von Tussle from *Hairspray*
- Mrs. Lovett from *Sweeney Todd*
- Mama Morton from *Chicago*

Objective #60: Make Yourself Study for the LSAT

Everyone reaches that point where they start thinking about taking the LSAT. You've been unemployed for four weeks, bills are piling up on the coffee table, and your parents are starting to talk about "making realistic plans" and "having to grow up sometime." At some point during this period, some well-meaning idiot will say, "Have you thought about law school?" as though it were a bold and unconventional solution. It's a stupid idea, but you've sunk low enough that you'll grasp at any straw, and law school is less stressful than dressing sores at a leper colony, and marginally more respectable than suicide. With that in mind, you pawned your Xbox 360 and used the money to register for the LSAT. You talked your father into "loaning" you the money for an LSAT study guide and actually went to the store and bought it, but that has been the extent of your preparation thus far. Now the book just sits there on the coffee table, gathering dust and mocking your feeble attempts to better yourself. You won't start studying without help, so use some mind control techniques on yourself to help.

Option 60.1: Power Tools
ABUSE/TORTURE

Make a deal with one of your friends to shoot you in the meat of the thigh with a nailgun every time you blow off studying. You won't need this to happen very many times.

Option 60.2: *Flash Card Cuties 7*
CLASSICAL CONDITIONING

Every time you sit down to work, accompany your study with graphic, hyper-explicit pornography. Soon, you'll get an erection at the very mention of the word "certiorari."

Option 60.3: Sleep Tapes
SUBLIMINAL MESSAGES/HYPNOSIS

Have your parents record an hour-long cassette talking about how of course they'll always love you, no matter what, but it would be much easier to if you'd get off your ass and make something of yourself. Play this tape while you sleep, while you're working out, while you're in the tub—basically, in any situation where you can feel shame. To be sure the tape is really effective, make sure your mother closes by saying, "No, we're not mad, just disappointed."

THE POVERTY CYCLE: OTHER STUFF YOU'VE PAWNED, AND WHAT YOU DID WITH THE MONEY

- Your racing bicycle: Paid half your cell phone bill so it looked like you were trying
- The silver cufflinks you got for graduation: Spent a night in a hotel to get a break from your actual, depressing life
- The gold watch you inherited from your grandfather: Enough Ramen noodles, canned baked beans, and off-brand sardines to last you through World War III or another six weeks of unemployment, whichever comes first
- Prescription sunglasses: An "Almost Armani" suit you wore to interview for a job washing cars; the job went to a one-legged Egyptian refugee who had prior experience

---

Objective #61: Get Access to Your Trust Fund

People always think it's so easy being an heiress, but it's harder than it seems. Sure, the astronomical fortune your parents have means you'll never have to work—actually, you don't even have to move, since you can easily afford to pay people to carry you from room to room—but it's frustrating not having control of your own money. Sure, you have an annual allowance that dwarfs the operational budget of Madagascar's government, but the bulk of your riches, all those lovely Krugerrands and mineral rights and that sixteen-pound tiara, is tied up in a trust. Your parents have indicated that they're willing to consider giving you full access eventually, but as things currently stand, they've said that it would be "irresponsible" to pass control of billions of dollars in cash and assets into the hands of a twenty-year-old girl who, as they put it, "didn't quite finish getting her associate's degree in alcohol poisoning at Wellesley." It's going to be your money eventually anyway; you might as well get your paws on it right away.

Option 61.1: A Heart as Golden as a Pre-Nixon Dollar

`LOVE-BOMBING`

Assuming your parents have some sort of conscience, they might be more likely to give you access to your trust if they thought you'd use the money for charitable purposes. Start founding charitable organizations, and go heavy on the schmaltz factor: If you can set up a self-sustaining situation where refugees from Darfur teach sick children how to train helper monkeys for disabled veterans who then help refugees from Darfur gain legal residency, you're on the right track. Whenever your parents express interest in what you're doing, sigh heavily, smile sadly, and say yes, it is nice, but you could do so much more if only you had more money.

Option 61.2: Sharper Than a Serpent's Tooth

`ABUSE/TORTURE`

Turn into one of *those* rich girls—the ones who do for upper-class American women what John Wayne Gacy did for clowns. Rise to prominence on the merits of a videotape of you vomiting during intercourse with a faceless man, and let your behavior degenerate from there. When your parents ask what it will take for you to stop embarrassing them so thoroughly, tell them it'll cost them a fortune—the fortune rightfully yours, to be exact.

THE PLAIN FACT: WHY YOU WERE SO ANNOYED YOUR PARENTS JOKED ABOUT YOUR HAVING AN ASSOCIATE'S DEGREE IN ALCOHOL POISONING FROM WELLESLEY

You have a bachelor's degree. In Egyptology. From *Mount Holyoke College*.

Objective #62: Get the Zookeeper to Let You Play with the Animals

You love going to the zoo. All of the animals fascinate you, but you're especially a sucker for the really cute ones. It's not a complete visit to the zoo until you've said hello to the slow lorises, the red pandas, the koalas, and all the other cuddlerific little animals they have. You just know those animals are great little snugglers. How could anything that looks so much like a baby Fraggle on Christmas morning not be? Unfortunately, you're barred from finding out firsthand because of zoo regulations, in the person of Clement, the sour-faced little zookeeper who watches your every move. You've tried asking him politely to let you play with them, but he just purses his lips and fusses about the animals' welfare. It's not like you want to eat them (although they're so damn cute you could roll them in whipped cream and jimmies and do just that), you just want to pet them and kiss their little faces. Fine. If Clement won't listen to your *perfectly reasonable* request, you'll have to find some other way.

Option 62.1: Become Part of the Tribe

`LOVE-BOMBING`

Every single day, spend as much time sitting next to the red panda enclosure as Clement will allow. Look at them, smile at them, and imitate their chittering little speech. After a few weeks, they'll come to accept you as one of their own. Once you're sure this has happened, leave. The pandas will miss you, and become listless and droopy. After they've sulked for a few days, Clement will come under pressure to get them to perk up so they're a draw for the zoo again. He'll have no choice but to call you up, apologize, and let you be joyously reunited with your little friends.

Option 62.2: Animal Rights

`ABUSE/TORTURE`

It seems hypocritical for Clement to claim to be so concerned about the animals' well-being, only to keep the lions and tigers from pursuing the thrill of the hunt. The patient lathe of evolution has shaped these cats into the most elegant, efficient predators the world has ever seen. Grab Clement and dangle him by the heels over the lion pit, just out of reach of their claws. If you do this in the middle of a Tuesday afternoon, no one will be around to see except kids skipping school, who won't bother you if you don't bother them, and Asian tourists, who will be reassured if you smile and wave. Let Clement hang there until he agrees to let you have Red Panda Time.

CULTURAL STUDIES: OTHER THINGS ASIAN TOURISTS FIND REASSURING

- Staying with the group at all times
- Giving the peace sign in photographs
- Large, clearly worded informational signs
- The presence of other groups of Asian tourists
- Photographing common items that do not differ in any obvious way from the ones in their home countries
- Timetables and the strict adherence to them

CHAPTER 7

72 VIRGINS, 99 LUFTBALLONS, AND ACCESS TO THE BUFFET

BRAINWASHING DURING WARTIME

The Chinese are often at the forefront of new military technology. In ancient times they built the aptly named Great Wall of China to keep out northern step invaders and to have a place to hang their erotic wood cuts; in the late ninth century they developed gun powder, becoming pioneers in the exciting new field of blowin' shit up; and a few centuries and some opium wars later, they invented brainwashing. Having spent the past several years convincing their own people to hang a portrait of Mao with skin cancer above their mantle, the Chinese realized they had a way with words and turned it to their advantage. Like previous Chinese inventions (see: fireworks; fried rice) brainwashing took the world by storm and is now a standard aspect of warfare.

Defense from our front line: And if you're appalled by our ability to make light of heinous war crimes, then you clearly haven't seen our off-off-Broadway take on a 1960s beach romp, *Waterboard Bingo Summer!*, which *Time Out New York* described as "uncomfortable as it is loud."

Objective #63: Get the Top Bunk

Oh, how unsuspecting you were when you came into the army. You always assumed your first battle would be against terrorists, communists, or at least hippies, but it turns out your first conflict after joining up was with a member of your own platoon. Ted seems to think he should get the top bunk because he "called it." In the civilian world, sure, that works, but not on the base. You've heard about the various exotic slithering critters that inhabit the Third World, and you'd rather have three more feet between you and them, but Ted is adamant. He called the top, he's on it, he's not moving. Well, fine. You have a few tricks up your sleeve.

Option 63.1: Start an Urban Legend

PROPAGANDA

Spread a new urban legend around the base that the top bunk is always the most dangerous. Fill in the details however you like: The army used a cheap contractor for the beds and the tops tend to just slide off, leaving the lower bunkmate unharmed; sometimes the blades fly off the ceiling fans and behead men in their sleep; Charlie always shoots up because the Vietnamese are so short. If someone tries to tell you that Vietnam is six thousand miles away, and that you're on a simple peacekeeping mission, shake your head sadly and say, "Oh, come on. Don't be naïve." After the rumors have had time to spread and get more intense in the retelling, Ted will be thrilled to switch places.

Option 63.2: Natural Disaster
GASLIGHTING/MIND GAMES

This one requires a lot of leg strength. Once Ted begins to snore, push up against the bottom of his mattress with your feet hard enough that it flips him out of bed. In response to his inevitable, "What the hell?!" sleepily respond, "Oh, that was a micro-tremor. Basically a tiny, localized earthquake. They have them all the time here. I grew up in California, so I'm used to them." Repeat as needed until he comes to realize that he just doesn't have the balance to be on the top bunk.

PSYCHOLOGY: WHY YOU REALLY WANT THE TOP BUNK

- The air circulates better up there
- At summer camp, you once had the bunk under a bed-wetter
- If you wake up from a nightmare and sit bolt upright, you won't smash your face on the bunk above
- You can masturbate without rattling the bed *as* much
- There's more room for your dream-catcher

Objective #64: Get Secrets Out of an Enemy Captive

It was much easier to capture an enemy combatant than you thought. The training had all these complicated instructions about tear gas and intelligence gathering and whatnot, and all you had to do was remember the old Wile E. Coyote cartoons. You simply dug a pit, covered it with some brush, and gently placed a Moon Pie on top of the piled sticks and branches. Well, what do you know? In about twenty minutes, here comes Charlie, ambling along, and as soon as he saw that Moon Pie, his eyes bugged out and he lunged for it. You let him eat the Moon Pie before you hauled him back to the base—enemy or not, he earned that dessert. Now you need to interrogate him, but you're not sure how to proceed. You still have all the waterboarding equipment, but when your commanding officer told you not to use it anymore, you couldn't tell if he had dust in his eye or was winking furiously to let you know to use the *fuck* out of the waterboarding equipment but pretend he didn't know about it. Well, it's there if you need it, but you might as well try some brainwashing first.

Option 64.1: Friendship

`LOVE-BOMBING`

Poor little guy. He's been captured, he's lost, he's probably frightened; he could use a friend. Give him some more Moon Pies and a few hugs, if that seems to be a thing in his culture. Make him feel like one of the guys. Then, once he gets comfortable, pry out his secrets the old-fashioned way.

"Truth or dare?"

"Truth."

"This is a two-parter. Do you have a crush on anyone here . . . and is there a chemical weapons factory on the main highway east out of Jalalabad?"

"Yes, and *yes.* Wait, I mean . . . shit."

> ### TESTIMONY: HOW YOUR CAPTIVE TRIED TO EXPLAIN AWAY HIS ANSWERS IN TRUTH OR DARE
>
> "Okay, wait. The translation is bad. I don't mean like a *crush*, I just mean he's *handsome*. Like, not a crush. Just, you know, I don't want to say no, I don't like anyone here, that sounds rude. Oh, and there's not a chemical weapons factory on that highway. It's a . . . it's a Dave and Buster's. It's not a very good one. The skeeball machines are all broken, and we can't get new parts because *someone's* government declared sanctions. Okay, but seriously, don't tell him I like him. I'm so embarrassed."

Option 64.2: False Flag
`GASLIGHTING/MIND GAMES`

Slip outside, change into native costume and a bandanna over your face, and then "break in" to "rescue" your prisoner. Check up on his condition as you lead him to "safety": "Did they torture you? Did you tell them anything, say, about a chemical weapons factory on the highway east of Jalalabad? I mean *I* know about that factory, since I'm on your side in this war, but I wondered if you told them what was made there, and whether it's still active."

Objective #65: Obtain Extra Rations

One of the most surprising things you discovered while adjusting to army life was how excellent the food was. You'd never have believed it, but reconstituted eggs, industrial fish product sticks, and factory carrots make for some good eating. You do have a complaint about the portion size, however. You understand that the powers that be want all you grunts to be lean, mean, fighting machines, but surely it can't hurt to allow second helpings . . . and maybe a little ranch on the side for dipping? If you're absolutely starving and don't yet have a black market source for Sour Skittles and Andy Capp's Hot Fries, use one of these manipulation tricks to cadge some extra rations from the mess hall.

Option 65.1: Parasites
GASLIGHTING/MIND GAMES

Sometimes, the only symptom of an internal parasite such as a tapeworm is an enormous appetite. If you're feeling especially bold, you can use your next furlough to pop over to India, drink some unfiltered tap water, and hope for the best. If you are pressed for time, you can forge a note from the base doctor stating that you do, in fact, have a tapeworm, and under new cost-effectiveness regulations it has been determined that it is, in the long run, cheaper just to feed the tapeworm along with the soldier instead of having you wormed like a colicky puppy.

Option 65.2: Fake Another Secret Mission
PROPAGANDA

Pass an anonymous tip along to WikiLeaks confirming that the CIA and United States Army are preparing to launch a daring commando raid onto Antarctica to claim it as the 51st state. "Operation Soaring Penguin" will allow American companies to plunder Antarctica's natural resources (ice for motel ice machines and seals to kill for meat and sell as "land salmon") and the Republican party to pick up three additional, potentially king-making electoral votes.

Once this revelation has had time to spread through the grapevine, approach the cook and tell him you have an order from "up top" to fatten up for a potential "very cold mission," so if he could save you some extra refried beans and shredded cheese, it would be appreciated.

GEOPOLITICAL RIPPLES: OTHER BENEFITS TO ANNEXING THE ANTARCTIC

- Endless supply of cheap penguins for American zoos
- Convenient base to spy on the Argentinians in case they get any more ideas about the Falkland Islands
- Additional land area might make USA larger than Canada, as the USA should be
- Will allow establishment of a polar bear colony so environmentalists will shut their damn yaps about disappearing Arctic ice for five seconds
- Susan Rice, U.S. ambassador to the United Nations, has been looking for an opportunity to moon the whole assembly since she got there, and even takes the stairs every day so that when the time comes she will have toned, taut buttocks

---

Objective #66: Convince Your Commanding Officer Not to Rat You Out Under "Don't Ask, Don't Tell"

In all fairness, you were told during basic training never to fraternize with the locals when stationed overseas, but you didn't think they really meant *Germany*. It's such a calm, reasonable place these days. Surely there's no harm in having a few drinks with some of the local boys—and, you know, if two or three of them happen to come back to barracks with you to play a few rounds of *Hiden der Schnitzel*, then that's just being neighborly. Unfortunately, your commanding officer got wind of your little adventure, and since "Don't Ask, Don't Tell" seems to be in place this week (stay tuned for local listings), you're in trouble. If you're going to be drummed out of the service, you'd rather it be for incompetence or coward-ice, not one night of Teutonic passion. Get Sarge to see your side of the story with one of these tricks.

Option 66.1: Secret Agent Man
GASLIGHTING/MIND GAMES

Although the built-in pun is groanworthy, you can always pretend that you were working on a deep undercover mission. As soon as you get into your commander's office, start talking before he has a chance. "Sir. I am pleased to report that Phase One of my infiltra-tion of the Berlin leather daddy community has proceeded with no unforeseen complications. I have gained the trust of several of its members, as I believe you saw, sir. It may not be a pleasant job, but we'll find out which one of them is leaking nuclear secrets to the enemy yet, sir!" He won't risk losing face by telling you he has no idea what you're talking about, and will let you go on your way.

Option 66.2: Truth in Advertising
PROJECT MK-ULTRA

Before going in to meet with the officer, douse yourself in Obses-sion for Men. If a reasonable amount is supposed to make you irresistible to the opposite sex, surely an enormous amount will make you irresistible to your own, and you can just sweet-talk your way out of the charges. Even if that fails, you may be lucky enough to have the fumes trigger a severe asthma attack—either for you or the officer—which will buy you a few days of thinking time while whichever one of you recovers in the hospital.

HISTORICAL CONTEXT: NOTED GAY MILITARY COMMANDERS

- Alexander III "the Great" of Macedonia: Conquered Greece, Egypt, the Levant, Persia, Babylonia, and countless men's hearts
- Richard I "the Lionheart" of England: Somehow, the other commanders of Christian forces during the Third Crusade weren't on board with Richard's idea that everyone should walk around naked to make the opposing Saracens too uncomfortable to fight
- Philippe, duke of Orléans: Louis XIV's brother wore makeup, perfume, and heavy jewelry when leading the French army against the Dutch, though this was not terribly surprising in seventeenth-century France
- Ernst Röhm: The leader of Nazi Germany's first secret service loved boys even more than he loved ethnic cleansing, but it was a tough call

Objective #67: Convince the Brass You're Competent Enough to Handle the Really Hardcore Weapons

When asked why you joined the army, you always make sure to talk about your family traditions, your love of home and country, and your hope that military discipline will craft you into a man of whom your mother will be proud. Secretly, though, you joined up for the same reason most people do: to be able to blow shit up with no legal consequences, and have the government foot the bill. Every Fourth of July, you were in charge of the fireworks, and every single year your science fair project involved something popping, bursting, overflowing, or exploding. Now you're in the army, and you'd think there would be bazookas and rocket launchers just lying around, but no. Apparently you have to pass "training" and "proficiency tests" and "competency drills" and "a thorough psychiatric screening." Even the Boy Scouts let you have knives and flares, but the military is punking out and fretting about "safety." If you just can't wait to do some taxpayer-funded wanton destruction, use one of these strategies to convince the brass you're a big boy who's ready for big toys.

Option 67.1: Super Soldier

`PROJECT MK-ULTRA`

If you truly appear to be "an army of one," it should make them more likely to let you use the really cool, advanced weapons systems. Pick up some human growth hormone on the black market and take a *dangerous* amount. Within a few weeks, the action of the hormone combined with the usual exercises one does in the service will make you a jacked, strapping he-man. Not only will you really look how a soldier should look, but the officers will also realize that they should take pains to protect the mighty war machine you've become. Let the cannon fodder defend themselves with plastic sandwich swords and potato cannons; *you're* too valuable to risk lightly, so you'd better have the heat-seeking grenade launcher.

Option 67.2: There's Always Hypnosis

SUBLIMINAL MESSAGES/HYPNOSIS

Polish your dog tags to a high sheen, then twirl them on your finger next time you're alone with your superior officer. As he slips into a trance watching the shining circle your tags trace in the air, have him repeat after you, "This young man is a real go-getter. When we need a red button pushed, he's the one to do it."

**EQUIPMENT MAINTENANCE:
HOMEMADE METAL POLISH**

Stainless steel and chrome can be polished with white vinegar. For an extra sparkle, mix the vinegar with a little baby oil, and rub whatever you're polishing with the shiny side of a piece of aluminum foil.

Objective #68: Get an Early Discharge

It's time to call it quits. You've had some fun chowing down on extra rations and blowing plywood targets to merry hell, but you never get any sleep because Ted, your bunkmate whom you outmaneuvered for custody of the top bunk, got a deviated septum during a hand-to-hand combat training session, and now he snores like six rutting moose fighting with chainsaws. You've tried kicking him so he changes position, surreptitiously putting nostril-opening strips on him as he sleeps, and taking fistfuls of Tylenol PM before bed, but nothing works; he just keeps a-sawing away. You requested to change barracks, but your request was rejected so quickly you didn't even have time to try to hypnotize the officer with your pocket watch. You have to get out of the army and get some sleep or you'll go sixteen kinds of apeshit. Since asking nicely won't work, try using a little mind control.

Option 68.1: Fake Sick

`PROJECT MK-ULTRA`

Save a small piece of meat from your dinner, let it spoil, and then eat it along with a healthy dose of hallucinogenic mushrooms. Repeat as necessary. After a couple of weeks, the medics will probably decide that your "attacks" of spewing vomit and gibberish are a drain on their resources to treat, and send you home to recover.

Option 68.2: Out–Jamie Farr Jamie Farr

`LOVE-BOMBING`

No one seems sure if "Don't Ask, Don't Tell" is still in effect, so put on a pair of cheap red pumps and stand outside the barracks asking each passing serviceman if he'd like to show a girl a good time, and count on the resulting awkwardness to grease the path of your application for early release.

Option 68.3: Go Mennonite

`PROPAGANDA`

Explain to your commanding officer that you've been reading some pamphlets the Mennonites were passing out, and you've decided to adopt their life of passive simplicity. As a newly minted conscientious objector, you will of course have to be released from your duties. If they demand to see the pamphlets, explain that, as many

Mennonites and members of similar groups spurn modern technology including industrial printing, they were handwritten on delicate autumn leaves that have since crumbled.

CULTURAL STUDIES: OTHER PERKS OF JOINING THE SIMPLE FOLK

- No pressure to keep up your carefully sculpted chinstrap
- You lettered in barn-raising in high school, and it's nice to keep your skills up
- You will never again have to watch a weakly cast romantic comedy struggle along under the weight of its own twee, gimmicky script
- A tranquil life of honest labor and peaceful joys
- Homemade jam!

Objective #69: Get the Military to Declare War on a Country You Don't Like

Well, well, well. If it isn't your old friend, the Bahamas. They think they can just deport someone for getting drunk and making a few bomb jokes at the airport and it's no hard feelings. Tough titties, Bahamas. They made you miss your cousin's wedding because of that interrogation in the secure area of Nassau International Airport, and you had a *really* clever speech planned in which you compared a happy marriage to a well-made batch of guacamole. (The husband is the avocado and provides a stable base, while the wife is the lemon juice and adds flavor and zest. It goes on.) Your probation might be over, but your fury at those *damn* Bahamians is not spent. Get back at them by starting a little war.

Option 69.1: False Flag

DESTABILIZATION

Learn how to fake a British Caribbean accent, then dress in shorts, a bandanna printed to look like the Bahamian flag, and an air-brushed T-shirt that reads "I'm from the Bahamas—what's it to you?" Dressed this way, start robbing convenience stores and casual dining restaurants all along Florida's east coast, remembering to shout, "You can't catch me! *I'm Bahamian!*" at the end of each heist. Soon, worry about the "Bahamenace" will spread to decision-making circles, and an embattled president will take action in a bid to boost his waning approval rating.

Option 69.2: Web Campaign

PROPAGANDA

Start a website detailing why you think it's reasonable to assume that al-Qaeda are hiding in the Bahamas instead of the mountainous areas between Pakistan and Afghanistan. Not only is it closer to the U.S. mainland, it's just generally a nicer place to be—would you rather hang out in a country where the national costume is an all-covering tarp, or where it's shorts and a sassy baseball cap? Plant these seeds of suspicion carefully, then wait as congressional pressure mounts to launch Operation Margaritaville.

INTELLIGENCE: THE NEXT SEVERAL COUNTRIES ON YOUR SHIT LIST

- Andorra: They have a revolting Christmas custom in which a magical log monster defecates candy
- Nigeria: They totally cleaned you out on one of those inheriting millions scams
- Finland: In high school, the Finnish exchange student fingered you after the spring dance, and then told *everyone*
- Eritrea: You bet $40 on them to win that little border skirmish with Ethiopia and they let you down
- Uruguay: "Well, lah-dee-dah! Look at me, I'm Uruguay! I enjoy a mild climate and a high standard of living! I have backward seasons and a little sun on my flag!"
- Panama: You're not over giving up the canal

Objective #70: Convince the Enemy They've Already Lost

This was a surprise. After your attempts to get the United States to declare war on the Bahamas succeeded, you assumed the Bahamians would put up a nominal struggle and then lie back and try to enjoy the whole process, much like you expected your Catholic prom date to do. Alas, no. Your prom date shouted, "Leave room for the Holy Ghost!" before socking you in the jaw with a solid right cross, and the Bahamians have been taking an even more direct route: They've been shooting at you. A lot. Apparently each of those tranquil, white, sand-fringed islands is home to at least one machine gun turret, and each of those smiling, relaxed natives is fully trained in marksmanship, Krav Maga, and "cutting a bitch up real pretty." Being practically between the United States and Cuba can put a country just a bit on edge, you now realize. As much as you dislike the Bahamas and all it stands for, you didn't want people to die during this little adventure; you just wanted some attention. Maybe you can skip the whole "fighting" aspect of this war and cut straight to the surrender.

Option 70.1: Sneak Attack
`GASLIGHTING/MIND GAMES`

The Greeks had the Trojan horse, the English had fire ships, and you have an eerie ability to mimic Ban Ki-moon, the current secretary-general of the United Nations. Have one of the tech guys hack into the Bahamian public address system, then hand the live mic over to you. Say, in your Ban voice: "People of the Bahamas. The Americans have left. They realized they were about to miss *Idol* and went home. The next armed forces you see will be United Nations forces. We are here to protect you, so please let us in. Pay no attention to the American flags stenciled on all our equipment. We're just borrowing it."

Option 70.2: Chemical Warfare
`PROJECT MK-ULTRA`

Intercept the next incoming shipment of rum. Open it and double the proof by adding grain alcohol, then reseal it and send it on its way. All the fruit juice in the punches they make will hide the taste of the extra alcohol, and a few hours after the next shipment comes in you should be able to just tiptoe in over their snoring bodies. When they wake up the next morning and demand to know how you all got to the capitol, answer: "Oh, man. You guys are gracious even in defeat. You threw us one *hell* of a surrender party. I'm not surprised you don't remember. You'd been pregaming pretty hard."

HISTORY LESSON: AWKWARD MOMENTS IN WAR

- 1204: Venetian forces en route to crusade in Holy Land stop in the Byzantine Empire, realize Holy Land is still far away; proceed to say "fuck it" and sack Constantinople
- 1871: The Paris Commune declares itself independent of France, forcing the French Republic to declare war on its own capital
- 1896: The Anglo-Zanzibar War lasts less than an hour in its entirety; Zanzibar is billed for the artillery it took to defeat it
- 1938: German army promises to put "just the tip" into Czechoslovakia; does not pull out for over six years

---

Objective #71: Organize and Implement a Successful Coup

Mounting a successful coup is one of the greatest challenges a brainwasher can face. Essentially, what you have to do is convince everyone involved to just give you a country, without fussing, "just because." It takes a lot of manipulation, all of which has to be brought off perfectly or the whole shebang comes crashing down, and you're just a common traitor instead of generalissimo and president-for-life. Follow the outline below to maximize your coup's chances of success.

Option 71.1: Gather a Band of Followers

GASLIGHTING/MIND GAMES

You can't quite do it alone. Using whatever network of contacts you've developed, spread a rumor on popular conspiracy websites that the current ruler is spending the contents of the national treasury on foul-mouthed prostitutes and hats made of silver-coated hedgehog pelts. Make it clear in the rumor mill that you, and you alone, possess the proof and also have the stones to confront him. After this tale has had time to circulate among the paranoid classes, issue a call to arms and have them meet you at a predetermined place. They may not be the best and brightest, but it's nice to have a group for the news photos and to draw rifle fire away from you.

Option 71.2: Convince the Current Leader to Leave Gracefully

LOVE-BOMBING

Nothing can turn a nice tidy coup into a big messy civil war faster than the previous leader escaping with a band of loyal followers and vowing to "fight till the end." Once you and your guards burst into his office, guns drawn, envelop him in a warm bear hug. Sit him on your knee, offer him a cookie, and explain that you're so, so grateful for all he's done for the country, but all good things come to an end. As a consolation prize, you're willing to pay the relocation expenses for his exile. A cozy little pied-à-terre on the Champs-Élysées will sound a lot better than squatting in a swamp surrounded by a bunch of unwashed rebels, and he'll probably be glad to leave quietly.

Option 71.3: Persuade the General Population to Accept Your Rule

PROPAGANDA

If the people of your target country are anything like Americans— and MTV International has ensured that they are—they'll be willing to forgive a celebrity anything. A few weeks before your coup, release a catchy dance single and star in an action movie where you fire off a lot of one-liners while saving a beloved national elder statesman from a ragtag alliance of the standard villains of the Third World mind: George W. Bush, the Mossad, Starbucks, and those *assholes* in the country next door who follow a different religion. They'll be so busy following your Twitter and Facebook updates that your rise to power will seem perfectly natural.

MEDIA: PROPOSED SUPPORTING CAST OF YOUR PROPAGANDA ACTION MOVIE, *ANTI-IMPERIALISM BLAST FACTORY 6000*

- George W. Bush: A bonobo whipped into a blind fury by electric shocks, voiced by Will Arnett
- Bumbling Mossad agents: Andy Samberg and Andy Samberg in a mustache, in an exciting dual role
- Starbucks executives: Dames Helen Mirren and Judi Dench, both of whom have tired of only playing queens and spies
- General foreigners: Stock footage of the Crown Heights riots, with obscene subtitles

CHAPTER 8

I'M NOT *NOT* GOD

CULTS FOR DUMMIES

Divine revelations happen in the most unexpected places: Paul had the road to Damascus; Buddha had a cozy spot under a banyan tree; and you had the banquet room of a local Sheraton during the cast party for *Noises Off*. After three star-studded weeks at the Knoxville Little Theatre, your run as stage manager was over and it was time to cut loose. Dehydrated from an hour and a half of selling it to the back row, you slam four cups of sherbet punch not knowing that the director had spiked it with mescaline in a misguided attempt to create a magical evening. Within moments, you were tripping even harder than your co-stars in that evening's on-stage pratfalls. Long story short, an angel appeared to you in the form of Lisa "Left Eye" Lopez and explained by means of puppets that you are the messenger of God. Ms. Lopez went on to say that you must work to build a pure society as an example to the nations. And practice safe sex. With that, she was gone and you had a mission. It won't be easy convincing people to join your "new religious movement," but you've got a few tricks up your sleeve.

Objective #72: Obtain a Rich Convert for Your Cult

Things are going swimmingly as you move into the second week of your new religion: You've made up some Gods, relying on stats from an old D&D book; you've refitted your shed into a "Temple of Oneness and Light"; and you got everyone on board wearing matching shorty terrycloth bathrobes (color-coded by rank). Unfortunately, you spent all the money you got from selling your plasma on beaded curtains and twinkle lights to give your temple that professional look. You could turn to your followers for help, but since you do most of your recruiting outside the methadone clinic, not only are they generally poor, they're not even eligible to sell plasma. It's time to secure your first rich convert. Most modern religions have a cash cow: California Buddhism has Richard Gere, Catholicism has Mel Gibson, and Judaism and Scientology divide the rest of Hollywood evenly. If you don't snag a rich convert soon—*at least* Carol Channing—it's just going to be you and the Wiccans fighting over change in the fountain at the mall.

Option 72.1: Earn Their Trust (Fund)
GASLIGHTING/MIND GAMES

Celebrities aren't the only people with more money than sense; the guy who invented the Swiffer has a daughter—and she just dropped out of Mount Holyoke College to "find herself." Find *her*. Talk a big game about peace and unity and oneness, and then casually mention that the initiation is a trip to Six Flags, followed by a drug-fueled orgy of truly Boschian proportions. Whether she's really a free wheeling Libertine or just wants to dismay *Fah-thuh*, if you're a good salesman, you'll pique her curiosity somewhere. If you can just get her back to the temple/shed, you're just a routine indoctrination away from getting her PIN number.

CONVERSION TIP: GOOD PLACES TO FIND IMPRESSIONABLE TRUST FUND KIDS

- A drunk tank in the Hamptons
- A deluxe hostel in Zurich
- Choate or collegiate graduation brunch
- On the south lawn, resting after an arduous round of croquet
- Loehmann's after a Scared Straight program
- At Betty's Babies rehab program
- In bed "letting their new nose settle in"
- A K-hole
- Backstage at a Jack Johnson concert
- Directing the servants in an amateur production of *No Exit*
- In bed with their stepmothers
- Purging

Option 72.2: We Think Her Name's Kassandra?

GASLIGHTING/MIND GAMES

Pull in one of the lesser Kardashians and build from there. Religions are just as trendy as anything else and if you can get her to tweet about it, you're made.

Objective #73: Get Corporate Sponsorship

You always promised yourself that you'd never sell-out and become one of those "corporate" cults like the Hare Krishnas or Judaism, but you also never knew how much toilet paper is needed for a compound of your size, or that your followers would be so insistent upon double-ply. It's starting to become apparent that you're going to have to compromise your cult's street cred slightly and find a corporate sponsor to keep you in Charmin. Fortunately, wife #17 (Moon Whisper, neé Arlene Kirsch) was friends with the VP of PR at Clearly Canadian in her former life and was able to get you some face time with the company to talk about sponsorship. *Unfortunately*, Clearly Canadian feels sponsoring a new religious movement would undermine their clear, refreshing reputation. Well, fine. You gave them a chance; now you're just going to have to brainwash them.

Option 73.1: Launch a Smear Campaign

PROPAGANDA

Clearly Canadian may be on their high horse (or in Canada, on their high *caribou*) about working with you, but at the end of the day, they are a business. Update your cult's website (www.geocities.com/nv5/Daves-Cult-Website_Final.com) with the plans for your mass exodus (or mass "suicide" if we're going to be sticklers about it) from Earth. Note that you're going to use Clearly Canadian Mountain Blackberry water (refreshes as it dispatches!) as the basis for your "exodus juice." If Clearly Canadian can make a wise business decision as well as they can refresh a thirst, they'll be quick to offer you sponsorship as long as you replace Clearly Canadian in the recipe with Formula 50 Vitamin Water.

Option 73.2: Convert the CEO to Your Cult

LOVE-BOMBING

With mailings, home visits, and the promise of a savior, you should be able to bring the CEO to your side. Besides, Canadians don't have a God—they have Anne Murray.

HOLDOUTS: CANADIANS' GODS YOUR RELIGION WILL HAVE TO COMPETE WITH

- Michael J. Fox
- Celine Dion
- Pamela Anderson
- Michael Cera
- A succession of mediocre stoner rock bands out of Vancouver
- Jason Priestley
- Shannon Tweed
- Rick Moranis

Objective #74: Get One of Your Cult Members to Leave

Don seemed like the perfect cult member when you converted him. He was socially awkward, attentive, eager to please, and had just gotten kicked out of the Coast Guard for 'schrooming during a mission. He's been at the compound for six months now, however, and it's been six months too many. He won't stop whistling Journey songs when he's working in the beet farm no matter how many times you tell him that the Divine Spirit is an Asia fan. He keeps forwarding you articles about how inhumanely the cows that produce Costco milk are treated and how the "family" should really switch to organic. He writes letters to the government on your behalf on *wide-ruled* paper. It's time to convince Don to try the National Guard before you decide you can't take it anymore and go back to Ponzi schemes and a part-time job at Kinko's like a normal person.

Option 74.1: Plant Patriotic Subliminal Messages

SUBLIMINAL MESSAGES/HYPNOSIS

Take his *Steve Perry: Greatest Hits* album and layer it with Toby Keith's "Courtesy of the Red, White, and Blue (The Angry American)." That way when he's toiling away in the beet field, he'll feel an irresistible urge to leave the compound and stick a metaphorical boot up somebody's ass via the U.S. armed forces. If not, there's always the possibility you've just created the next big mash-up club anthem and will need to fly to Berlin to DJ a Svedka vodka party. So either way: damn good day.

Option 74.2: Torture His Inner Animal Rights Activist

ABUSE/TORTURE

Organic milk, *'eh?* Well, if it's organic milk he wants, it's organic milk he'll get. Get a cow—preferably the cutest cow that money can buy—and set it up in a barn within sight of Don's beet field. Next, go to Bed Bath & Beyond and buy the sturdiest reaching tool they sell (we prefer the Gopher Deluxe, but to each his own). Every day when the cow is not being milked (and hell, maybe even when it is being milked), stand about four feet away from it and repeatedly administer light pokes to his hindquarters with the reaching tool while staring deeply into Don's eyes with a look that adequately expresses, "You did this, not me." The cow might be slightly annoyed, but Don will be devastated. How could he have believed in a religion that sanctions animal cruelty? Hopefully he'll ditch you, bypass the military completely, and join PETA. (Now *there's* a cult with its shit together.)

KNOW YOUR ENEMY: HOW DON GOT KICKED OUT OF THE . . .

- Army: Refusal to cut his luxurious chestnut locks to anything shorter than a graduated bob
- Air Force: Delivered a note to his master sergeant from his mother in flowery script explaining that Don has a severe peanut allergy and thus can't fly with the "rest of the boys"
- Marines: Three words: Big Ol' Queen

Objective #75: Get One of Your Cult Members to *Stay*

Whoa, whoa, whoa, let's not go throwing around the *P*-word all willy-nilly. No, not *that* *P*-word, you pervert. Try to remember this religion is based on good, clean Christian values. (And a slurry conversation you had with God one night when you were robo-tripping your ass off, but mostly Christian values.) Nobody on your compound is a "prisoner," and members are free to come and go whenever they feel like it. But come on, disgruntled apostate, you can't leave *now!* You just got here! And we're gonna play Bananagrams later! And we just made a fresh batch of margaritas! And . . . and Mike just got here! Everyone loves *Mike!* No? They still resent being restricted to a diet of Ikea meatballs and Clamato juice and hate sharing a bed with two pit bulls? Well, that's fair enough, but you can't just give up on them. Would Paris give up on Helen of Troy? Would Uncle Sam give up on Lady Liberty? Would the padlock on the front gate give up on keeping everybody riiiight where they are? No. So you should probably make Disgruntled Apostate think that cult life is a barrel of laughs, because she's not going anywhere for awhile.

Option 75.1: Music Therapy

SUBLIMINAL MESSAGES/HYPNOSIS

Did you ever notice that it's physically impossible to be in a bad mood when you're at Disney World or Disneyland? (Or Euro Disney, for that matter.) (Well, maybe not Euro Disney.) That's because the park is covered in hundreds of strategically hidden loudspeakers pumping peppy Muzak into the park to subconsciously make you want to get happy and try the churros. Take a page from Mr. Disney's book and duct tape a few boom boxes around the walls of your compound blasting your infamous "Dave's Funk Mix 1." This idea is of course also steeped in the psychological theory that it's hard to be unhappy when you're too busy getting down with your bad self.

OTHER MIXES DAVE ROCKED THE PARTY WITH

- "Ska's the Limit!"
- "Count Davcula's Halloween Jams"
- "Gone But Not Forgotten: The Best of Luther Vandross"
- "Dave's Funk Mix 2"

Option 75.2: Move Your Compound to a Bad Neighborhood So Everyone Is Too Scared to Leave

DESTABILIZATION

We hear land in Oakland is cheap.

Objective #76: Write Your Doctrine

As much as your beloved apostates wish it weren't true, you can't *always* be there to show them the way. Even the reincarnation of Jesus Christ occasionally needs to take some "me time" and take the phone off the hook, slip into the tub with a glass of Pinot, and forget all about the archangel of death descending upon earth in his space sled pulled by fifty screaming virgins to drink the blood of the infidel. Unfortunately, it's hard to concentrate on your guided visualization tapes when the flock keeps text messaging you question after question after question. "Wait, we pray to what in the direction of where now?" "Do we believe in a grasshopper heaven?" "Are homosexual *thoughts* a sin, or just acts?" Since the average member of your cult seems to have the focus of a Ritalin-deprived seventh-grader recently hit over the head with a banjo, it might be a good idea to actually write some of this shit down. You've been meaning to do it for years, but writing is such a bore. God wanted you to be His *messenger*, not That Guy who spends all day in Starbucks listening to Wolf Parade and working on his "screenplay." If you want to whip up a religious text but need to be done before *Fringe* comes on at nine, use a brain-washing shortcut.

Option 76.1: The Time Saver

GASLIGHTING/MIND GAMES

The Anglican Communion seems to produce some consistently dedicated followers, so get a Book of Common Prayer, cross out each of the "Her Majesty the Queen, Supreme Governor of the Church of England's," and crudely write in "Dave the Kick Ass Leader" in Sharpie. While you're in there and already desecrating holy texts, you might want to go ahead and scrap that entire part about women and modesty because we don't know if you've seen, but Moon Whisper has got some *ankles* on her.

Option 76.2: The College Approach

PROJECT MK-ULTRA

Wash down a couple of Adderall with a sugar-free Red Bull, type "When in doubt— *dance!*" into a new Word document, blow it up to 72-point font, fudge the margins, and turn it in three minutes before the deadline.

FOR YOUR REFERENCE: CULT ORIENTATION DAY 1

- 8:30 A.M. – 9:00 A.M.: Continental breakfast
- 9:15 A.M. – 9:30 A.M.: Welcome remarks
- 9:30 A.M. – 10:30 A.M.: Icebreakers
- 10:30 A.M. – noon: Seminar: "So What the Heck are the Rules, Dave?"
- Noon – 1:00 P.M.: Box lunch (provided)
- 1:15 P.M. – 3:00 P.M.: A coordinator walks new members through how to transfer all of their money into the "cosmic departure toll" account
- 3:00 P.M. – 4:00 P.M.: Robe fitting
- 4:00 P.M. – 5:00 P.M.: Trust exercises
- 5:15 P.M.: Shuttle departs

Objective #77: Make Your Followers Think You're Charismatic

It takes a very specific kind of person to be a successful cult leader. Not just any Tom, Dick, or Harry with kind eyes and a value-pack of Kool-Aid can pick up a wizard's staff and get anyone to sail away with him on the *S.S. Wingnut*. Studies show that the most crucial attribute of a successful cult leader is a charismatic personality. Charisma is that certain *je ne sais quoi* few people possess that makes them able to attract, charm, and ultimately control just about anybody they want to. It's the difference between being "Micah's racist uncle with the 'stache" and "Führer of Germany." Unfortunately, you are not a charismatic person. The last time you said something charming was in 2007 and actually you were just reading aloud from an inspirational magnet in Bed Bath & Beyond. You articulate like a human Mad-Lib ("Oh you know, he's that guy with place and the thing and the common household object") and have the self-esteem of the only girl at fat camp without a date to the final weigh-in. If you want to keep your followers from dropping you the minute the Branch Davidians open a local franchise, use one of these mind tricks to turn yourself into a charmer.

Option 77.1: Mic Yourself

PROPAGANDA

People all too often confuse being charismatic with being loud. It's easy to own the room when you spent the entire dinner party shouting titty jokes through an empty paper towel tube and shaking a pair of maracas. Outfit yourself with a headset microphone turned up to the max volume and try your hardest not to startle yourself the first time you speak. If a follower asks what's in your ear, just say it's your Bluetooth phone and hope he finds assholes charming.

> **FOR YOUR REFERENCE: WHAT YOU SHOUTED THROUGH THE EMPTY PAPER TOWEL TUBE**
>
> "What's the difference between Carol and my bitch ex-wife? At least Carol thanked me for the pearl necklace!"

Option 77.2: Become a Ladies' Man

`SUBLIMINAL MESSAGES/HYPNOSIS`

What do Bill Clinton, JFK, and Idi Amin have in common? They were all charismatic leaders and they all got more play than an acoustic guitar in a frat house. Hire a harem of "working girls" to be your arm candy around the compound, and your followers will subliminally think you must be seductive and powerful. (They don't have to know you go back to your room and just talk.) (And yes, those women do charge you just to talk.)

Objective #78: Get a Journalist to Write Complimentary Things about Your Cult

You put one little photo of you and your "wives" wrestling on the cult's website and suddenly you're being interviewed in your shed/shrine by Chuck Klosterman for a ten-page exposé in the April issue of *Esquire*. You weren't sure if you should let Mr. Klosterman in on the intimate details of your cult (or "novelty religion," as you should probably refer to it around him) or not. On one hand, this could be an amazing opportunity to defend your beliefs to thousands of people and prove that not all "alternative religions" are led by dangerous Nike-clad stereotypes. On the other, you sleep in a tin foil hat so Tim Allen doesn't steal your dreams. It was a real Sophie's Choice. In the end you decided to take part in the exposé to see if at the very least you can't get a few more Twitter followers for the cult account out of it @Savior4U_98. (Ten more and you tie The Moonies!) Now that it's actually happening, however, you're starting to think that you may have made the wrong decision. You didn't come this far to end your career as a *B*-side in *Sex, Drugs, and Coco Puffs II*, so brainwash the journalist to go easy on you with one of these.

Option 78.1: Inundate Him With an *Absurd* Amount of Praise for His Work

`LOVE-BOMBING`

In a time when blogs are suddenly the preferred source of news and entertainment, and prestigious magazines are folding like Jimmy Carter with a pair of threes in Texas hold'em, freelance journalists have been better. Odds are he'll be so moved you actually appreciate his well-honed craft ("It's like, I didn't get a master's from Northwestern's prestigious Medill School of Journalism just to work for something called a *Drudge Report*, you know?") that he'll feel obligated to return the favor.

Option 78.2: Build Your Own Potemkin Village

`GASLIGHTING/MIND GAMES`

Legend has it that when Russian general Grigory Potemkin wanted to trick Catherine II into thinking that the Crimea totally had its shit together, he draped a few backdrops from the *It's a Small World!* ride over the desolate riverfront, lit a scented candle, and told everyone to "act cool" when she sailed by. Do (essentially) the same thing. Hire slightly better fed actors to play the part of your followers for the day. Hang an "out of order" sign on the door to the gunroom and tell him "Sorry, john's on the fritz again." Put the kibosh on any and all harbinger-of-death talk for the day. If he doesn't see smoke, he won't look for fire.

READING MATERIAL: SELECTED CHAPTERS FROM *SEX, DRUGS, AND COCOA PUFFS II*

- "Bareosmith: My Trip to a Nudist Camp with Steven Tyler"
- "Bratz, Otherness, and the Decline and Fall of Western Civilization"
- "Super Soothe Me: The Month I Only Drank Pepto-Bismol"
- "Phish and Chips: When Hippies Gamble"
- "Leaving Flowers in Our Wake: A Month on the Road with SHeDAISY"

Objective #79: Get Your Followers to Take the Worship Down a Notch

It's understandable why you wanted to be worshiped. No matter how many e-cards your grandmother sent you saying otherwise, you've never felt very special. All that changed though when you started your own cult. Now when you walk through a room, people genuflect instead of politely excuse themselves to go check on the roast. Getting to sit through your rant on "Why We Shouldn't Have Let Germany Stay a Country" is a reward for good behavior and not what ruined a perfectly good brunch. People continue to avoid eye contact, but now it's out of respect and has nothing to do with your sty! You thought you'd never want the party to end, but recently things have started to get a little overwhelming. It's gotten to the point where you never have anything to wear because cult members keep stealing your shirts "just to smell you." Last Halloween, everybody went as the same thing—Dave. (Except for one girl who went as "Slutty Dave.") Not one but *two* of your followers have a backpiece featuring you as a centaur. It's weird. And when the person with a goblet of ghost tears on their nightstand "for salvation emergencies" thinks something's weird, you know it's really, *really* weird. If you want to get your followers to back off but don't want to lose them in the process, use one of these manipulation tips to get them to loosen their own cords.

Option 79.1: Tell Them God Said So

GASLIGHTING/MIND GAMES

"Oh, oh man, you guys. So I was lying in bed last night watching old reruns of *Silver Spoons* when The Higher Being totally flew out of my TV and manifested Himself in the form of Alfonso Ribeiro *right* in front of me. I know, it was crazy. So anyway, He was like, 'Oh, hey, Dave. You're doing a really good job here on Earth as my son or messenger or whatever it was I originally told you you were, but you know what would make me *really* merciful and stoked in the afterlife? If maybe you and the rest of the flock started establishing some healthy boundaries and learning that a relationship with limits is normal and doesn't necessarily mean that you're a failure or anybody is about to leave you, because guess what? I'm not your father, so stay out of my fucking *closet*. I mean, so stay out of each other's fucking closets. Okay. Well. Peace be with you and such and such.'

And then there was this huge flash of light and he was gone. I know, crazy. So . . . Yeah, I'm just gonna go up to my room and take a nap now and I, uh, I guess you have to stay down here and not crawl in later to hold me because, you know, *He sort of said so."*

Option 79.2: Make Them Think You Have a Horribly Contagious Disease

GASLIGHTING/MIND GAMES

Slap some peanut butter and corn flakes all over your body, say, "Damnit, leprosy's acting up," and enjoy being worshiped from afar.

PARAPHERNALIA: OTHER THINGS ON YOUR NIGHTSTAND

- A bottle of Tylenol PM
- A copy of *How to Win Friends and Influence People*
- A dream journal
- A framed Glamour Shot of Moon Whisper
- A ring from where you put the goblet of ghost tears down without a coaster

---

Objective #80: Get Your Friends to Join Your Cult

The first rule of molding someone into a first-class cult member is that you have to remove them from their daily life and isolate them from their friends and family. It may sound a little harsh, but who needs those turkeys when they have you and an exciting new career in competitive childbearing?! To set a good example, you practice what you preach. (Well, except for that whole part about taking the third day of each month to sit in a bathtub of Zima and reflect on charity. At that point you were just trying to see how far you could go before someone would call bullshit.) You live on the compound and keep yourself just as cut-off from society as the rest of the flock. While it's nice to be a small-business owner and set your own hours, and save the world from certain damnation, it's also kind of lonely. Your followers are nice enough, but they can't fill the void left in your heart by your friends back at home. Nobody could. You tried inviting the old gang to join your cult, but apparently living in an abandoned summer camp in the Ozarks with fifty of the sweetest ex-Juggalos you'll ever meet is "not even an option." If you can't risk breaking your own rules by sneaking them in, but they'd still rather drink their own piss than try Faygo, get them to reconsider joining with one of these options.

Option 80.1: Tell Them the Compound Gets Free Beer
PROPAGANDA

Then when they get there, explain that you accidentally waved your arm and turned the beer into Clearly Canadian, and then let the crisp, refreshing flavor of British Columbia do the rest.

Option 80.2: Perform Some "Miracles"
GASLIGHTING/MIND GAMES

Get a magic kit, take your friends somewhere mystical like a clearing at dawn or a . . . cornfield, turn a few threes into fours, and hope they're *real* stupid.

FOR YOUR REFERENCE

Examples of Convincing Miracles

- Walking on water
- Rising from the dead
- Curing lepers
- Stopping the sun in the sky
- Ascending into heaven

Examples of Unconvincing Miracles

- Turning raw food into cooked food using only a microwave
- Aging a year in only 364 days
- Removing facial hair with a single strip of wax
- Holding your breath for "almost" thirty-four seconds
- An erection

Objective #81: Get Your Flock to Shore Up the Population

There may be twenty-four usable hours in a day, but only so many of them can be spent handing out pamphlets and pens in front of the Wash-A-Teria. Sometimes you just have other shit to do. Do you think the original Jesus Christ spent every one of his waking moments on Earth hustlin' for the Lord? He was a go-getter, sure, but the Man was also human. He had library books to return and expired driver's licenses to renew just like the rest of us. If evangelism has to take a back seat every now and then but you want your cult numbers to continue to grow, it may be time to encourage your members to embrace their holy responsibility and be fruitful and divide. But first things first: you gotta get them in the mood.

Option 81.1: Slip Spanish Fly Into the Food Rations

PROJECT MK-ULTRA

Spanish fly (actually a small, green beetle) is said to be one of
Mother Nature's most powerful aphrodisiacs. Farmers grind Spanish fly to use the powder to get animals to mate, while humans
have been slipping it into each other's cocktails and hoping for the
best since the fifth century B.C. A healthy portion of Spanish fly in
the compound's food rations should be all it takes to get your followers in the mood to *"spread your message,"* if you know what we
mean. Just don't use too much because there's a fine line between
an effective dose and a toxic dose, and Wikipedia doesn't specify
where that line is.

Option 81.2: Visual Stimulation

SUBLIMINAL MESSAGES/HYPNOSIS

Movie nights on the compound are generally reserved for screen-
ings of the shorts you made that summer you were really into *Wal-
lace and Gromit* and briefly considered a career in Claymation, but
it's time to switch things up. Dim the lights, pour some wine, and
let a suggestive movie do all the heavy lifting. The movie should fall
somewhere between *I'm Not Rappaport* and straight-up porn—in
other words, a 1980s titty movie.

AUDIO/VISUAL AIDS: MOVIE NIGHT ON THE COMPOUND

- *The Bikini Carwash Company*
- The *Angel* Trilogy
- The *Porky's* Trilogy
- *Revenge of the Nerds* 1–4
- Pretty much any movie featuring a character named Boner, Woody, or Chet

CHAPTER 9

THANK YOU, SIR, MAY I HAVE ANOTHER?

STOCKHOLM SYNDROME AND YOU

1973 was a busy little year. Roe v. Wade led to an abortion boom; Richard Nixon, jowls aquiver with indignation, assured the country that he was not a crook; Marvin Gaye made everyone uncomfortable with the soul hit "Let's Get It On"; and a six-day hostage crisis in Sweden brought public attention to a controversial behavioral theory called Stockholm syndrome. Stockholm syndrome is a psychological phenomenon where hostages begin to side with their captors. The most famous example of Stockholm syndrome is the case of newspaper heiress Patty Hearst, who was abducted by the Symbionese Liberation Army and eventually helped them rob a bank. Whether you're a captor, captive, or just planning a delightful jaunt to Sweden, Stockholm syndrome is always the joker in the deck.

Objective #82: Rid Yourself of That Hostage Still Hanging Around

Your eleventh-grade math teacher, Mrs. De Kander, would be surprised to know that not only did you live up to your potential after all, but that it took no trigonometry whatsoever to take a few people hostage, ransom them, and use the money to fund your new life in Brazil. Sines and cotangents be damned; all you needed was a Super Soaker full of cat pee, a Junior League tea full of women in expensive dresses, and a city council that was surprisingly receptive to your demands. Now you're off to sunny Rio (first class, Mrs. De Kander), with a briefcase full of cash (unmarked, nonsequential bills, Mrs. De Kander) that will easily serve as seed money for the business you've always dreamed of: an erotic bakery that uses only organic, locally sourced ingredients (with gluten-free options, Mrs. De Kander). There's just one wee fly in the ointment, in the person of Alan, the event waiter you brought to the airport handcuffed to you to make sure the authorities behaved until you were in the air. You tried to set him loose at the duty-free shop, and even offered to buy him some booze as a no-hard-feelings gesture, but he seems to have developed a nasty case of Stockholm syndrome, and has grown attached to you. Now he's sitting next to you, filling up on free champagne, gently stroking your arm, and saying things like, "When *we* open *our* organic erotic bakery, I think *we* should use shaved chocolate to make pubic hair." It's flattering in its own way, but it's gone far enough. Here's how to handle your new, undesired best friend.

Option 82.1: The Mile High Club, Sort Of

ABUSE/TORTURE

Lure him into the airplane lavatory with promises of an intimate moment, then sucker punch him. Alert the stewardess that there's some unconscious dude hogging the bathroom.

Option 82.2: Alcohol, Righter of Wrongs

PROJECT MK-ULTRA

Brazil is home to more than appalling poverty, Carmen Miranda, and the world's best asses. It's also the birthplace of cachaça, a brutally potent liquor that can, in a pinch, be used to run a gasoline engine. Once you land, take Alan out for a drink to celebrate "new beginnings." And another to celebrate "fresh starts." And another to celebrate "a promising future." Once he starts gently swaying, even when seated, place him in a cab. Tell Alan he's going to "the hotel," but quietly instruct the driver to deposit him at the embassy. Hopefully, the embassy will take its role as lost-and-found depot seriously and send Alan home faster than you can say, "It's not you, it's me."

USEFUL TOOLS: OTHER UNORTHODOX WEAPONS FOR A HOSTAGE TAKING

- A sock full of nickels
- Wicked hangover breath
- Grape juice ("So help me God, I will stain this rug!")
- Five honey badgers in a burlap sack
- "Third-degree" Indian burns

Objective #83: Stop a Hostage Who Is Adding an Uncomfortably Erotic Element to the Whole Thing

You'd think librarians would be well educated, but not one of them can tell a paintball gun from the real thing. You couldn't do more than bruise them and add a wacky, '80s-style splatter pattern to their clothes, but here they are, cowering, pleading, and agreeing to your demand that they stock back issues of large-print *National Review*. This was almost too easy—you'll never write a strongly worded letter again. You'd like to stay here, ranting madly about the "liberal media" and "huggle-snuggle Great Society pantywaists" until they throw in *The American Spectator* as a goodwill gesture, but Irene is posing a problem. When you came in, she was dressed in a high-necked blouse, long skirt, bun, and owl-shaped brooch— you know, like a librarian. As the "incident" has progressed, how- ever, she's unbuttoned her blouse to the navel, ripped the hem of the skirt to create a provocative slit, unfurled the bun, and pried out the rhinestones that formed the owl's eyes and affixed them to the corners of her own eyes with spit for a sassy look. She has also wrapped herself around your leg and said, "I see your rifle, but where is your gun?" It's not that you're not interested; it's just that this is about thought-provoking conservative periodicals, not about getting to third base with some Dewey Decimal doxy. Here's how you can put Irene back on the shelf.

Option 83.1: Recruitment

LOVE-BOMBING

Try to convince Irene to join The Cause. Give her her own paint- ball gun and have her take over the library in a nearby town. Tell her that you'll be happy—nay, honored—to couple with her once every library in the land stocks *National Review* and Barry Goldwater is on the six-dollar bill, but until then there's no time for fraternization.

Option 83.2: Kink

`PROJECT MK-ULTRA`

Pretend to be into it, but insist on using correction fluid as emergency poppers and hope she's as much of a lightweight as she looks.

Option 83.3: You Do Have a Weapon

`ABUSE/TORTURE`

Shoot her with the paintball gun a few times. It'll blow your cover, but nothing will dampen her ardor faster than several raised welts in a frowny-face shape.

FOR REFERENCE: OTHER MEN WHO HAVE INADVERTENTLY UNLEASHED THE EROTIC FORCES UNEASILY CONCEALED BEHIND IRENE'S BLAND EXTERIOR

- Robert Bork, failed Supreme Court nominee
- Ed Asner, TV's Lou Grant
- Rajiv Gandhi, former prime minister of India
- David Duchovny, niche heartthrob for weird girls
- Kyle, the guy who restocks the snack machine (which ensures an awkward scene every other Friday)

Objective #84: Stop Falling in Love with Your Captor

Oh, wow. Someone would have to be pretty smart to find his way into this top-secret military research facility you work at. It's especially incredible to realize that, even as Gustavo and his splinter group were planning this raid, he still made time to go to the gym and build biceps like you've never seen. It's not that you consider power or danger an aphrodisiac . . . It's just that he's right there, screaming, waving a gun around, and you haven't been this aroused since Larry Hagman took his shirt off in a rerun of *I Dream of Jeannie*. He's making a lot of sense, too. Of course we should give Maine to the Palestinians. Of course you can't get cancer unless you believe in it. Of course the federal government invented Native Americans to have a cover story for the casinos, the profits of which are used to pay the heavy tribute our alien overlords demand. It's all so clear now—as clear as Gustavo's unflinching, commanding gaze. Oh, Gustavo . . . Not to be judgmental, but are you fucking kidding us? You're on the verge of wrapping yourself around a terrorist like ivy? Ignoring the whole "treason" aspect, do you really want to spend every date night from now on dressing in a baggy East German surplus kit and egging the Jewish Community Center? Brainwash yourself out of a life plan that will end in your most embarrassing court date yet.

Option 84.1: Hurt Yourself

CLASSICAL CONDITIONING

Get the stapler—the good one—and every time you look at Gustavo and start to get lost in his warm, inviting, bugged-out brown eyes, drive a staple into the meat of your thigh. Keep doing this until you associate him with stabbing pains instead of a wonderful life together.

Option 84.2: The Black Widow

LOVE-BOMBING

This may be your only chance to combine extreme sexual transgression with a bid for the Presidential Medal of Freedom. Lie back on your desk and start murmuring about how your Stockholm syndrome seems to be focused on the red-light district. Once Gustavo takes the opportunity, get him through the eye with a check spindle and win one for the Gipper.

GOOD EXAMPLES: OTHER NOTABLE FEMMES FATALES

- Judith: Ancient Israelite woman who seduced Holofernes, general of the Assyrian army that threatened Ancient Israel, then cut off his head and got her own book in the Bible
- Marie Antoinette: "Of course we can afford it. We're the King and Queen of France. What are they going to do, break open the prisons, behead us, and plunge Europe into decades of war? Don't be a chickenshit."
- Susanna Dickinson: The "Yellow Rose of Texas" seduced the Mexican general Santa Anna, allowing the Texan forces to attack during his male refractory period and win Texas's independence from Mexico
- Monica Lewinsky: The Syrian army made twelve tons of nerve gas while we were all distracted by the half-assed games of "anything but" she played in the Oval Office

Objective #85: Encourage Stockholm Syndrome to Make Your Captives More Tractable

Now, it's not that you're losing sight of the ultimate goal. You still firmly believe that Utah and Nevada should be combined into a single state, Nevtah. Both states could merge their individual modest electoral vote totals to create a double-digit, kingmaking powerhouse. The staid, family-friendly attractions of Salt Lake City and the freewheeling roulette-and-whores belt of Nevada lend themselves easily to the tourism slogan of the new state, "Something for Everyone!" And forty-nine stars just do fit better on the flag, Hawaii be damned. You still believe in The Cause, it's just that last time, when the plan was to make Arizvada and the group took over Flagstaff's Meteor Crater Visitor Center, none of the captured forest rangers liked you. Everyone else kind of . . . you know, paired up with a hostage. Even the guy with coprolalia, who sporadically shouts, "Booger! Fuck! Rugmuncher! Asshole!" and was brought into the group to seem inclusive, became buddies with the receptionist. You were clearly the odd man out, and the hostages could tell. They never listened to you. Make sure you're not the wallflower next time, when you take over the Cowboy Poetry Hall of Fame in Elko.

Option 85.1: Feel the Burn
ABUSE/TORTURE

Love is blind, arguably, but you're not shooting for love. Psychosis can see, and it likes to see a toned physique. Start hitting the gym. It won't be pleasant by any means—this method is coded as "torture" for a reason—but the better you look, the more likely it is your captives will start doodling "Mrs. Gun-Toting

Hostage-Taker" on scraps of paper. While you're at it, start using a moisturizer and get a haircut other than the wedge you've had since 1998.

Option 85.2: Win More Flies with Honey than Vinegar

LOVE-BOMBING

You win more flies with honey than with vinegar: Just because it's a hostage situation doesn't mean good manners don't count. Say "please" and "thank you"—the "or I'll break your feet" is implied by the nunchucks you're carrying. Schedule regular bathroom breaks and crack open the glass front of the snack machine so everyone can have their choice. Most hostage takers are rude; stand out by being a class act.

HELPFUL HINT

Remember, confidence is everything. Charles Manson was as ugly as homemade sin even before the jailhouse swastika forehead tattoo, but he had confidence. He also kept his sights reasonably low: ever see a picture of Squeaky Fromme or Leslie Van Houten? "Who Would You Rather . . ." has never been so high-stakes.

Objective #86: Explain to Your Wife That It's Not Cheating If You Had Stockholm Syndrome

Every marriage goes through rough patches. Money, work, kids, sex, the nightmarish realization that your spouse is going to be in your house for the rest of your life, watching old Hepburn/Tracy movies with her mouth slightly open and stacking one more used coffee filter on the top of the trash instead of just taking out the damn bag like someone who was raised in a *house* instead of a guano-filled cave . . . These things can strain a relationship. So can infidelity, regardless of whether it was technically "your fault." You've tried carefully explaining the situation. You were at work, minding your own business, when in barged an enraged woman with a Tupperware container full of scorpions, demanding that the insurance company pay to have her deviated septum fixed. You tried to explain that she was in the sales office and she really needed to take this issue up with claims, but she kept yelling, "*Listen!*," inhaling really hard (and, granted, there was an audible whistle), and shaking the scorpions to enrage them. You were frightened at first, but then . . . confused. And then, well, as it turns out, that woman's septum wasn't the only thing deviated about her, but it didn't count! It's not cheating if you had Stockholm syndrome, just like it's not gay if you pretend the other guy is Anna Kournikova! Make your wife understand.

Option 86.1: "Oh, Mr. Sheffield!"

PROPAGANDA

Fran Drescher works in mysterious ways. Screen for your wife the pivotal episode of *The Nanny* in which Fran is taken hostage in a bank and ultimately convinces her captor to add a designer dress to his list of demands. "See! Fran Drescher did it to an actual robber! And this woman had scorpions! You know how unsettling I find things that skitter!"

Option 86.2: Tit for Tat

ABUSE/TORTURE

Hire a very attractive man to take your wife captive, strip down to a cock sock, and gyrate until she realizes that *accidents happen*. Make sure he's in on the back story so he doesn't take it too far, leaving you either a widower or caught in an endless round of "No, it's *my* turn to be an erotic hostage."

WHEN TO KEEP YOUR MOUTH SHUT

Under no circumstances should you note that, as it turns out, the woman who burst into your office neglected to poke any air holes in the lid and had in fact burped the Tupperware, so the scorpions were logy to begin with and dead by the time you got your trousers back on.

Objective #87: Use Stockholm Syndrome as an Excuse to Get Out of Work

Hopefully, when this book comes out it will sell enough copies to change all this, but at the moment people almost never use Stockholm syndrome as an excuse. Don't you think everyone's tired of the same threadbare old excuses involving Title IX, Agent Orange, and the fact that you've never really gotten over Roxie Roker's death? Don't you think your boss would appreciate the clean freshness of "I'm sorry I didn't show, I was too busy identifying with my attackers"? Your boss will know you're lying—you set a bad precedent with: "I still miss Roxie. Because of the agility her experience playing high-school sports taught her, she was able to keep me from falling into a puddle of Agent Orange." But it's never too late to earn points for originality. Before you start claiming to be Lenny Kravitz's godfather, try one of these options to escape nine-to-five for the day.

Option 87.1: Skipping Work to Watch a Marathon of *Maude*

CLASSICAL CONDITIONING

"Bea Arthur looks a lot like my paternal grandmother, who sent me a telegram the third of every month to tell me that tubby little crybabies like me would never grow up to be the first astronaut president. When Bea smiles during the opening credits of *Maude*, I almost . . . almost feel like Grandma loves me."

Option 87.2: Skipping the Office Christmas Party

LUDOVICO TECHNIQUE

"I don't like talking about this, but when I was sixteen I worked as an elf for a seasonal Santa display at a department store, and it turned out to be a front for a group of Satanists. I was drawn in. My parents ultimately rescued and deprogrammed me, but whenever I see a lot of Christmas décor it makes me crave a chalice of goat's blood."

WHAT THE SATANISTS RENAMED THE REINDEER

"Thrasher, Necromancer, and Slasher, and Nixon! Comet (striking the Earth), and Lupus, and Dahmer, and Blitzkrieg!"

Objective #88: Determine If One of Your Captives Has Fallen in Love with You, Or Just Has Stockholm Syndrome

Well, this is embarrassing. You and your friends stormed into the Italian consulate, brandishing *American Gladiators*–style foam battle mallets, planning to occupy it by force until the Italian government agreed to end its occupation of Ethiopia, only to discover that the Italians had in fact already made plans to evacuate Ethiopia. And completed them. In 1944. (It appears that the library's atlas may be the wee-est bit out of date.) Your friends are ready to leave; they're tired of social justice–themed birthday parties, and would rather return the mallets and use the money to run to the liquor store. You're willing to admit that this raid was as big a failure, in practical terms, as your benefit Ice Luge for AIDS St. Patrick's Day bash, but you're hesitant to leave. Giuseppe, a nice young man who appears to be some kind of especially sensual file clerk, has been passing you sweet little notes since the beginning of the incident. His spelling is frankly terrible, but the sentiments are tempting and the little drawings of Cupid are highly accomplished. You're interested, but worried. Does he like you for you, or just because you're his captor? Is it love . . . or is it Stockholm syndrome?

Option 88.1: Catch and Release

LOVE-BOMBING

Remember the lizard you caught and wanted to keep when you were five? Remember the patchouli-drenched stoner boyfriend you had when you were twenty? Remember the surprisingly sound greeting-card advice your mother gave you on both occasions? "If you love something, set it free. If it comes back it's yours to keep; if it doesn't, it was never meant to be." Lower your weapon and move from between Giuseppe and the door. If it's just Stockholm syndrome, it will probably wear off and he'll bolt.

Option 88.2: Act Normal for Once

PROPAGANDA

So your relationship started because of Stockholm syndrome. That doesn't mean it has to end there. Take Giuseppe on a nice date—at mallet-point, if need be to maintain the romance—and convince him you're worth a weapon-free date. Tell him all about your rough childhood, your struggle to get your GED while holding down a job selling lists of phone numbers to Nigerian princesses, and your rewarding career training monitor lizards as comfort animals for shut-ins. Show him that the woman behind the mallet is every bit as alluring as the mallet-wielding lunatic that bopped him mercilessly four hours ago.

EVENT PLANNING: OTHER ILL-ADVISED IDEALISM-THEMED PARTIES

- North and South Korea Speed Dating to Speed Reunification
- Enough Candy for Everyone: Serbs, Kosovars, and Piñatas!
- India Versus Pakistan Curry Cookoff (Especially unhelpful: referring to the spiciest category as "nuclear")
- All-You-Can-Eat Buffet Benefit for the Hungry

Objective #89: Get Your Life Back Together After Being Acquitted of Hostage Taking

You're free! After four hours and two minutes of deliberation ("To be honest, we were decided before lunchtime, but the county provides a generous meal allowance, and none of us had had Red Lobster in forever"), you're a free man. You've been acquitted of a series of crimes, including, but not limited to, the theft of a beige 1978 Dodge Dart, head-butting a meter maid who "had a lot of attitude for an agent of the imperial-fascist world regime," and mailing a small box of cat feces to every member of the United States Congress except Olympia Snowe, who seems sweet. The jury bought your attorney's argument that you had Stockholm syndrome, dating from your abduction by a left-wing terrorist group posing as a college show choir known as the "Red Refrain." Now that you're off the hook, how do you put your life back together?

Option 89.1: Make It Your Schtick

CLASSICAL CONDITIONING

Granted, she was already rich, but it still totally worked for Patty Hearst. Once freed, she got to be in some John Waters movies, see her name in trivia games and crossword puzzles, and have a standing invitation to any talk show. Try being "the Stockholm syndrome guy." Side with the rude cashier at the chicken place—the one who always tells your wife she "looks like she has enough thighs." Call the police when your mother runs a yellow light. Cheer for the New England Patriots. Be that guy.

Option 89.2: Sell Yourself with the Frantic Enthusiasm of a Panamanian Houseboy with a Webcam and a Dream

`PROPAGANDA`

While your case is in the news, accept any and all interview offers. During interviews, cry for most of the time, thank God every four minutes, and remember to talk about how it brought your family together. Invest the interview fees prudently and retire to one of those hot countries that don't get American newspapers very often.

PUTTING IT ALL IN CONTEXT: OTHER GEOGRAPHICALLY NAMED MENTAL ILLNESSES

- Jerusalem syndrome: A mild, transient psychosis sufferers experience when overwhelmed by the spiritual heritage of Jerusalem (mostly suffered by Japanese tourists)
- Paris syndrome: A mild, transient psychosis sufferers experience when overwhelmed by the artistic heritage of Paris (mostly suffered by Japanese tourists)
- Tampa syndrome: "I don't know, dude, ever since I moved to Tampa I've worn sleeveless, airbrushed T-shirts; put my Natty Light cans in neon-colored, sexually explicit Koozies; used Sun-In every day, even though I'm a man and it's not 1987; and had like ten restored Oldsmobile 442s repossessed."

Objective #90: Recapture Your Captor's Interest After All These Years

Time flies. It seems like yesterday, not twenty to thirty years with credit for time served ago, when you walked into that Chinese restaurant and everything changed. No sooner had you sat down when that angry young man burst in, armed to the teeth, demanding all the money in the cash register—and, though he didn't know it yet, your heart. It was love at first "shut the fuck up and I won't freak out," and the two of you spent a glorious thirty-six hours together, eating fortune cookies and talking about everything and *anything*. As the police dragged the two of you away from each other, your captor promised that he'd never forget you and would do everything in his power to hunt you down the minute he got out of jail. This romantic gesture was ultimately misinterpreted as intimidating a witness and ended up getting him five extra years, but still, it was from the heart. Recapture the magic now that he's being released.

Option 90.1: Moral Relativism

PROJECT MK-ULTRA

When he arrives, immediately offer him a hot, refreshing cup of cocoa and Rohypnol. Under any other circumstances at all, this would be inexcusable wickedness, but your courtship began with a burst of M-16 fire. You're not playing by society's rules, and haven't been for a while.

Option 90.2: That Certain *Je Ne Sais Quoi*

ABUSE/TORTURE

Men like a woman who can still surprise them, even after years have gone by. When your erstwhile captor knocks at your door, answer wearing only a sexy, enticing negligee . . . and brandishing an Uzi. Keep him captive for a few days, alternating pistol-whips with caresses. After a week or so, he'll be as crazy about you as you are crazy. Stockholm syndrome started this relationship, and Stockholm syndrome will see that it endures.

TRACK LISTING OF THE MIX CD YOU MADE YOUR CAPTOR

- "Stand by Your Man," Tammy Wynette
- "He Hit Me (And It Felt Like a Kiss)," versions by The Motels, The Crystals, Hole, Frank Rogala, Grizzly Bear
- "Every Breath You Take," The Police
- "I Will Always Love You," Dolly Parton
- "You Were Meant for Me," Jewel
- "(Everything I Do) I Do It for You," Brian Adams
- "Reunited (And It Feels So Good)," Peaches & Herb
- "Bad Case of Loving You," Robert Palmer

Objective #91: Get Your Ex-Captor a Prison Care Package

Nuts. Despite your tearful testimony that your captor, Eli, had your full consent to hold you at knifepoint for three hours in the Long and Wide section of the local Payless Shoe Source, the judge ruled that you had Stockholm syndrome "or some kind of menstrual derangement," and that your testimony was to be disregarded. The jury subsequently convicted Eli, to your enormous dismay. You just know he's going to hate prison. Someone with such a tender soul will wilt under the pressure of group showers, rehydrated mashed potatoes, and no reading materials except old Michael Crichton paperbacks with obscene flipbooks drawn in the page margins. You can't break him out of prison until you get a better lead on where to lay hands on some napalm—it can't *all* be locked up, can it?—but you may be able to get him a care package with some treats and essentials. Prison being prison, however, you can't just mail it or walk in on visiting day holding a gaily wrapped package aloft and shouting, "Here comes the Easter Bunny with a special surprise for a special felon!" You'll have to smooth the guards to let you deliver it intact.

Option 91.1: Nothing to See Here
`CLASSICAL CONDITIONING`

Every time you visit the prison, bring a comically oversized box holding only a few pieces of candy for the guards. During your visit, calmly break the box down and throw it away. After the guards get used to the fact that you enter with a box and leave without one (and come to look forward to your offerings of Fun Size Whoppers), add a false bottom to the next box and stock the top with candy as usual. Then in the visiting room, instead of throwing the box away, deposit it where Eli can get to it, and leave empty-handed as usual.

Option 91.2: Exploit the Liberal Media
`PROPAGANDA`

Write letters to every acronym-named rights or public advocacy group you can think of, explaining the injustices involved in Eli's predicament. One of them will take the bait—if all else fails, try the ACLU, the St. Jude of leftist hissy fits. Once the story gets traction, after a few protests at American embassies in Europe and then a Barbara Walters special, look for the prison guard wearing a "Malia Obama/Dennis Kucinich 2016" pin and ask him if he believes in freedom, and if he's willing to take a risk for justice.

MATERIALS CHECKLIST: THE CONTENTS
OF ELI'S CARE PACKAGE

- Twenty small sandwich bags, each containing a single serving of Goldfish crackers
- A selection of Ken Follett's sweeping, dramatic historical fiction
- Some old issues of *High Society* and *Oui* (men have certain . . . needs, and once he's done he can use the pages like cash)
- Candy corn (loose)
- Enough C-4 to "probably" blast a hole in an exterior wall
- A Game Boy that still works, but the Donkey Kong cartridge is stuck in it
- Easter grass

CHAPTER 10

BLUE JEANS AND COCA-COLA

DEPROGRAMMING

You can find a greeting card for nearly every occasion. Ruin your niece's bat mitzvah? "You are now a woman—woman enough to forgive me?" Friend's pet died? Choose from the extensive "Gecko Heaven" collection. Is your cousin having a rough menopause? Brighten her day with a card featuring two retired ovaries sunning themselves on deckchairs. And yet not even Shoebox Greeting Cards offers a "So Your Loved One Was Brainwashed" line of condolence cards. There's a reason for this. As evidenced by the past nine chapters, brainwashing is a subtle art, as elegant in its ways as calligraphy. An expertly manipulated mind is a work of art; if you wouldn't put pasties on the Venus di Milo, you shouldn't undo a well-done brainwashing. But if it's absolutely necessary, be responsible, do it right, and follow our advice.

Objective #92: Re-Educate Your Commie Toddler

You were so grateful to get little Timmy out of your hair for the summer; city children need fresh air, and city parents need to go on the occasional week-long bender. It seemed like a great idea to send him to Red Hills Summer Camp ("Where children learn the value of sharing, hard work, and team sports!"). Now that he's back, however, it's become increasingly clear that Red Hills wasn't named after the distinctive North Georgia landscape, but after a certain little book. He came back knowing how to play "The Internationale" on the recorder, he keeps spelling "bourgeois" on the refrigerator in his magnetic letters, and he brought a bust of Lenin for show and tell. You need to put an end to this before he starts asking Grandma for May Day presents. Your mother is a Christian woman; she won't know where to find fair-trade Pop Rocks and a children's illustrated *The Communist Manifesto*.

Option 92.1: Uncle Sam and Ice Cream

CLASSICAL CONDITIONING

Make sure they understand that in your family, privileges are for capitalist little boys and girls. "Well, we're taking your sister out to get ice cream, but I guess since the cows don't get a cut of the profit, you'll want to stay home and clean your room." "No, you can't take a 'mental heath day' on the day of the President's Challenge Fitness Test; you'll need to be strong for the Revolution." "Oh no, we won't be going to Disney World this year—that's exploitative. You can spend your spring break in the basement playing Belarus. Leave the lights out and then it'll feel like a brownout."

Option 92.2: Hollywood Therapy

`LUDOVICO TECHNIQUE`

Dress him in his sister's star-spangled gymnastics unitard, plop him down, and make him watch *Big Business, The Associate,* and *Dora the Explorer's First Investment*. Really, any Whoopi Goldberg movie will steer you in the right direction. If you think about it, *Sister Act* is really about self-sufficiency—and *Sister Act 2* is McCarthyism propaganda at its best.

FORCED DETENTION: OTHER CHILDREN'S PROGRAMS APPROPRIATE FOR DEPROGRAMMING

- *Big Bird Gets All the Toys Because He Has More Money*
- *SpongeBob Made-in-a-Sweatshop-Overseas Pants*
- *Teenage Mutant Ninja Consumers*
- *Mr. Rogers' Gated Community*
- *Kids Incorporated*
- *Pooh Denounces Piglet to the House Un-American Activities Committee: It's Painful, But It's His Duty as an American*

Option 92.3: Pyongyang Shuffle

`ABUSE/TORTURE`

Cut your losses and trade him for a North Korean child who didn't fit in because of his admiration for Reaganomics.

Objective #93: Re-Homosexualize Your Lover Who Got "Fixed" at Gay Therapy Camp

You know it's normal for people to change and evolve during a relationship. A little spare tire around the mid-section, the odd donation to Ron Paul, a sudden interest in artisanal salad dressings—all par for the course, sure. But when Terrance went away to "The Right Direction," it turns out it was less of an orienteering conference and more of a reorienting process. Terrance has now moved into the basement of your shared modest split-level ranch-style home where he sits all day eating Cheetos and desperately trying to understand ESPN. He looks at women on the Internet, but he's not up to speed on the latest trends and thinks that Kathy Ireland in a sports bra and pair of bicycle shorts is the epitome of "just fabulous." To feel more masculine, he blasts Korn at full volume, thrashes around his room, and shotguns Miller Lites; but every time he just ends up having a panic attack and needing you to rub his back while he does his "breathing exercises." You haven't just lost a partner, you've gained an asshole roommate. But if they straightened him out, you can bend him back again.

Option 93.1: Make Him Watch an Endless Amount of Gay Porn

LUDOVICO TECHNIQUE

You know when you hear a song you haven't heard in a while and you totally forgot how awesome it was? Well, that's kind of what you're trying to do here. Except instead of "Pour Some Sugar on Me," it's hardcore gay pornography. Next time he's doing his "breathing," take advantage of his guard being down and hogtie him. Throw him in front of the biggest TV in your split-level and queue up a series of the most graphic "films" the local adult store has to offer. He may cringe at first, but by the third straight hour of wall-to-wall sodomy he'll be nostalgic for the good ol' days.

Option 93.2: Turn His Basement Into a Frat House

`DESTABILIZATION`

He wants to be a straight man? Well, dial that shit up to eleven and turn his cozy basement into a disgusting, frat-tastic sty. Clog the toilets (with whatever is convenient); keep no food in the house except baking soda, Jägermeister, and canned ravioli; institute a "pissin' corner"; pick up the odd drunk sorority girl and leave her in an inconvenient place in the house, like the stairs; and blast Blink-182—24/7, 365. He might last about a week before he collapses in your arms and begs you to run the Swiffer, but probably not.

DESTABILIZATION TRICK: PLACES TO LITTER DRUNK SORORITY GIRLS

- In a dryer
- On the coffee table
- Propped up against the pantry door
- Curled up around Terrance's arts and crafts box
- Asleep on the pull-out ladder to the attic
- Atop Terrance's sleeping form
- The toilet

Objective #94: Wean Your Mother Off Home Shopping TV

Night after night, she sits there, the flicker of the television reflected in her bifocals. You find her in the morning, slumped wherever she fell asleep, the cordless phone in one hand and a bank card in the other. It started the year she had gout and couldn't go Christmas shopping; now she does it every night, buying gifts for the eventual weddings of children still in the womb and birthday presents for everyone in her graduating class, even the exchange student who is now the Labor Minister of Finland. She's promised to stop, but she hasn't. The house is filling up with food dehydrators, acne treatment systems, reversible jewelry, and packing peanuts. Every item she owns is Euro-Oxy-Hydro-something, a revolutionary new _____ not available in stores. You worry that one day you'll stop by with some flowers and find her little body crushed under a pile of NutrOxySystem, a slow cooker that pipes oxygen bubbles onto the food, which somehow reduces the appearance of fine lines and age spots while repairing your credit score. You have to stop her.

Option 94.1: We Love You and We Want to Help You

LOVE-BOMBING

Nothing is more passive-aggressive than an intervention. You get to talk behind someone's back before the meeting, cry on purpose, and use the phrase, "We love you, but . . .," all the while claiming that it's "for her own good." Shopping has joined drinking, using drugs, having sex, eating, and cutting oneself as an addictive behavior with its own TV show. Call in the cousins and the bridge club and hit Mom across the chops with a two-fisted blast of tough love.

Option 94.2: Margarita Madness

`PROJECT MK-ULTRA`

Take Mom out to lunch, and encourage her to enjoy a cocktail or two. When she's in the ladies' room, turbocharge her drink with a shot from your emergency grain alcohol supply. On the way home, as Mom's eyes lose focus and she starts belting out Motown standards in a smoky alto, stop by a judge's office and ask if he could squeak in a competency hearing before golf. It's not that hard to be awarded power of attorney over a woman who uses the judge's ornamental scales of justice as a microphone for a rendition of "He's a Rebel."

CORPORATE PUBLICATIONS:
HOW THE NUTROXYSYSTEM WORKS

Food loses oxygen during cooking. The NutrOxySystem replenishes this oxygen, making it stale *to the untutored palate* but ensuring that you get the FDA-recommended 40 grams of edible oxygen each day. The rejuvenating energy of the oxygen stimulates the pituitary gland, causing it to release hormones that produce collagen, resulting in a more youthful appearance. Youthful people are confident people, confident people are successful people, successful people have good credit scores. QED.

Objective #95: Reconvert Your Sister from Dave's Cult

Victory! After a daring daylight raid, you've rescued your half-sister Aileen from an organization called "Dave's Cults, Candles, and Beets: Come for the Beets, Stay Because Seven Archangels Are Riding a Comet Toward Earth, and When They Arrive They Will Eviscerate the Sinful with Flaming Swords." You've tried explaining to her that she's free, that she doesn't have to worry about having to go back, and that she can go back to being the Christmas-Easter Episcopalian she used to be, but no dice. She just sits at the table in her shortie bathrobe, carving beets into floral shapes by the light of a hand-dipped candle. She occasionally reminisces in a wistful tone: "Moon Whisper and I were going to French braid each other's hair. I guess she's stuck with that unflattering ponytail now." It would all be terribly sad if it weren't so stupid—and, frankly, ungrateful. You went to a lot of trouble to rescue her, and here she sits, leaving beet peelings on the floor and sighing, without so much as a "thank you." Before you get so frustrated you just send her back, try a couple of brainwashing methods to snap her out of it.

Option 95.1: Calming Slaps

ABUSE/TORTURE

It works in the movies—you know, someone finds a body and starts screaming and hyperventilating until one of the other characters hauls off and slaps her and she settles down. You may have to belt Aileen a number of times, since that cult is apparently wedged pretty deeply in her consciousness. Think back to the time she tattled on you for eating all the Life Savers out of Mom's purse and you got grounded, and slug away.

MOTIVATION: OTHER THINGS AILEEN DID THAT MAKE YOU GLAD TO HAVE AN EXCUSE TO SLAP HER

- Walked in on you in the bathroom and shouted, *"Mom! Jason's having puberty!"*
- Blamed every single fart on you between 1993 and 2006
- Made fun of your associate's degree in General Studies
- Drove Dad to the bottle
- Had enough money to backpack around Ireland, but not to buy you a graduation present

Option 95.2: Something Stronger

LUDOVICO TECHNIQUE

Aileen can't be particularly strong-willed if she converted to the beet farm religion. If God is on the side of the strongest battalion, surely Aileen is on the side of the nearest God? Sit her down in front of a *700 Club* fundraising marathon and let Pat Robertson work in obnoxious ways, his wonders to behold. By the sixth time one of the female hosts cries mascara-blackened tears after hearing a story about the power of prayer, Aileen should be convinced. You might get tired of her endless choruses of "Jesus Wants Me for a Sunbeam" and her tendency to be slain in the spirit at the dinner table, but at least she won't be sulking anymore.

Objective #96: Cure Your Daughter of Bieber Fever

You've been dreading something like this for the past year, ever since your wife informed you that your beloved daughter Nora had recently received her inaugural visit from the uterine lining fairy. She was ready to discover boys, and the teen-marketing corporate juggernaut anachronistically known as "the music industry" had already begun matchmaking. With Justin Bieber's likeness stamped on jewelry, woven into beach towels, plastered on billboards, and drawn among the clouds by talented skywriters, it was only a matter of time before your daughter's still-timid ovaries drew her toward this smooth-faced, unthreatening little waiflet with the floppy hair and unblinking eyes. It's a relief to see that her dawning sexual awareness still has its training wheels on, but in the meantime she's turned the house into a cult-of-personality shrine exceeded in the thoroughness of its devotion only by Graceland and North Korea. Even China under Mao would have been easier to take; in his pictures, Mao usually looked out into the glorious future of the revolutionary motherland, but "the Bieb" gazes right at the viewer, with the soul-piercing directness of an Orthodox icon. Before the FBI shows up at your door because an IP address registered to your house looked at every single result for the Google search "justin bieber shirtless," cool her ardor with one of the strategies below.

Option 96.1: Father Knows Best

CLASSICAL CONDITIONING

To a teenage girl, nothing is more embarrassing than having parents. It would be far less shameful for her to have a mass of writhing tentacles in place of legs than to admit she was spawned by a man who buys Michelob Ultra in bulk. Every time your daughter mentions the Bieb or looks directly at his image, call one of her friends and announce that Nora has a father named James, who is a 39-year-old tax attorney and loves his daughter so much it renews his faith in God. She will *quickly* learn to associate the two events, and wean herself off her crush before everyone finds out she has anything as awful as a *dad*.

Option 96.2: Scare Tactics
GASLIGHTING/MIND GAMES

At night, as she sleeps, shift all of her Bieberphernalia nearer to the bed, facing directly at her, and tint the eyes faintly red. Do this nightly, drawing the items ever nearer and making the eyes redder and redder. If she has any sense, by day four she'll pitch it all in the bonfire and douse the ashes with holy water.

TIMELINE: OTHER DEVELOPMENTAL HURDLES TO LOOK FORWARD TO AS NORA TODDLES TOWARD AND INTO ADULTHOOD

- A conversation in which Nora asks to go on birth control just to help clear up her skin, and you and your wife assure her that you trust her. All of you will be lying.
- You will overhear her confiding to a friend that she went to second base, and you will spend the next week deliberately not imagining what "second base" is to a generation that sends naked photographs in text messages in high school.
- Nora and her mother will have a battle royale in Dillard's while shopping for a dress for the ninth-grade dance; the catalyst will be when your wife points out that a low-cut dress doesn't make sense on someone who does not yet have much to reveal.
- Nora's best friend will call you because Nora got too drunk at a house party and needs to be picked up. On the way home, she will vomit so hard that the next day you will find a half-digested almond in the ashtray.
- She will marry beneath her, and you will never be able to say so.

Objective #97: Diversity Training

You thought nothing of it when your husband's great-grandmother invited your young son to stay with her in the family house in Greenwich, Connecticut. It would be nice for Brendan to see another part of the country, and—not to seem insensitive— Grandmother Ward-Smith does have a lot of money, and it would be nice to keep Brendan in the forefront of her mind in case she should happen to revise her will. He had a wonderful time, and came back full of stories about his trip. Unfortunately, several of the stories reveal that Grandmother Ward-Smith has several . . . no longer popular ideas, which she seems to have transmitted to Brendan. He's labeled the downstairs bathroom "For Colored Use Only," tried to keep the cat from playing with the Siamese next door, and refused to wear green on St. Patrick's Day because "it really wouldn't do to be seen acting Irish. Not for one of us, dear. They steal, you know." You tried to remonstrate with him and explain that in your house, he would treat everyone equally, but he laughed and said, "Oh, come now, Mother. The natives love having the Europeans in charge because they're too distracted looking at each other in loincloths to run the country for themselves." He's even copied some of Grandmother's mannerisms; it's disturbing to see an eight-year-old boy clutch his pearls and sniff haughtily. Before he starts a major incident by tipping the mailman a nickel, take action.

Option 97.1: Desiree's Baby

DESTABILIZATION

Take Brendan aside and explain that it hurts your feelings when he talks about other races because your father was black. Give him a few seconds to realize that this means *he's* part black, and to ask you if you're sure he's a quadroon. Reply, "Oh, goodness no. Quadroons are three-quarters white, and my grandmother on the other side was a Parsee with a Cherokee mother. I'm also fairly certain your father's Chinese." Ruffle his hair and walk off.

Option 97.2: Oscar Bait

LUDOVICO TECHNIQUE

Sit Brendan down for a marathon screening of *Crash, Mississippi Burning, Beloved, American History X*, and any other movie that inspired you to send a donation to the United Negro College Fund. He may come away hating white people, but at least you'll be able to take him to Taco Bell again.

THE FACTS:

The United Negro College Fund provides college tuition for African-American students and also helps fund scholarships at private Historically Black Colleges and Universities. The late, great soul, jazz, and blues singer Lou Rawls led the organization's annual fundraising telethon, "An Evening of Stars," from 1980 until his death in 2006. For more information, or to donate, visit *www.uncf.org*. Consider sending a donation today. *Do it for Lou.*

Objective #98: Get Your Drinking Buddy Back

Rob was never really an alcoholic, in your opinion—he just liked to drink. Some people play bridge, some people restore classic cars, and some people, like Rob, add a little Kool-Aid mix to a handle of Banker's Club vodka and drink the resulting "thinkin' juice" while making prank transmissions over the ham radio. It was all good clean fun, until the night that a misunderstanding about "Prince Albert in a can" led to the surprisingly efficient Monégasque secret police raiding his house. As part of the deal reached in order to avoid escalating the incident, Rob had to attend a number of court-mandated Alcoholics Anonymous meetings. It was funny at first, but over time his resolve seems to have weakened. He's come by your house six times to make amends to you, recently filed a sex-discrimination lawsuit against the Women's Christian Temperance Union, and is melting down his collection of Mardi Gras beads to produce more sobriety tokens. You also understand that Monaco's foreign policy is still crippled by the prevalence of Princess Grace conspiracy theories, but enough is enough. Your loud, abrasive drinking buddy had become a loud, abrasive advocate for respon-sible decision-making—it's as though Gilbert Gottfried joined the Promise Keepers. Get your friend off the wagon with one of these strategies.

Option 98.1: A Bunch of Hypocrites
`DESTABILIZATION`

It won't do any good to trick Rob into drinking again. That would just make him go back to the beginning, apologize again, and show you his 24 Hours sobriety token again while remarking, "This is the hardest one to earn." What you can do, though, is sneak into the meeting room before hand and Irish up the contents of the obligatory coffee machine. When Rob arrives and sees his sponsor belting out a slurry rendition of "Sweet Sue" as an arm-wrestling tournament takes shape in the background, he'll be so astounded at the hypocrisy that he'll be more than eager to go in halvsies with you on a keg of Natural Light.

Option 98.2: The Spuds MacKenzie Method

LUDOVICO TECHNIQUE

Joe Camel and friends have been turned out to pasture with restrictions on tobacco promotion, but alcohol advertising is alive, well, and effective. Create a mix of all the commercials showing beer's connection to bikini-clad women jiggling their way along on speedboats and monster trucks, and place it in the DVD player in lieu of Rob's cautionary tale of the day, *The Lost Weekend*. The only thing that persuades a man faster than a 600-horsepower engine is a tit, and you've got them both right here.

FUN FACT

The Women's Christian Temperance Union is still active today, despite the decline of temperance politics. Its members are not only opposed to alcohol but also to all illegal drugs, tobacco, same-sex marriage, and abortion. Their headquarters are regularly toilet-papered by the League of Women Voters.

Objective #99: Get Your Dad to Stop Watching Anime

After thirty years serving as cantor at several area synagogues, your father expressed a desire to "sit on my tuchus and watch all the movies I've missed. That's why I ate all those blintzes, so I'd have a nice soft tuchus to sit on when I retired." At first, he watched fairly standard fare, annotating each film with zesty commentary. Then, somehow, he found *My Neighbor Totoro*, and everything started to change. The bright colors, the strange motion, the delightful whimsy . . . *something* struck a chord in your dad, who proceeded to watch the movie six times that very day. By the end of the week, he had spent four hundred dollars at the video store on Japanese animated features. Six days later, when you stopped by to say hello, your father was seventeen hours into a *Mermaid Privacy Rodeo* marathon. He had on a set of cat ears, and what hair he had left was dyed electric blue. As you gaped in horror, your mother said, "*Do* something. He wants us to go to something called a 'con.' I had to tell my mahjong group we had scarlet fever." You'll see what you can do.

Option 99.1: Create an Incest Taboo

CLASSICAL CONDITIONING

Make sure that a pornographic anime winds up in his "to watch" stack; he doesn't need to watch it all, just enough so he realizes that many of them are extremely graphic. After this seed has been planted, start showing up at the house in a too-tight sailor suit with half the buttons undone and with your hair in pigtails. Once his mind creates the following neural pathway

Anime → girls in ill-fitting uniforms → having sex with an octopus ⇢ daughter

he won't ever be able to look at it again without a shudder.

Option 99.2: Make a Man Out of Him

PROJECT MK-ULTRA

Our bodies change over time. It's possible your father is running low on male hormones, so pick up some "testosterone enhancement blend elixir" in Chinatown and dose his coffee with it until he goes back to *Die Hard*.

QUOTABLE: DAD'S ZESTY COMMENTARY

- *What Women Want:* "He had to have a drunken nervous breakdown before everyone realized he was a yutz? Did no one see this? He's wearing pantyhose!"
- *Waterworld:* "Just let me drown if this happens. I'm too old to drink urine, I don't care how it gets processed."
- *Titanic:* "Now, Jews aren't efficient people. It took us forty years to cross the Sinai, but I'm telling you: Spielberg could have wrapped this up in under two hours."
- *Scream:* "People joke about Jewish parents being overprotective, but look at all those little gentiles getting stabbed. You knew to call one of us if you were at a party and people started drinking or stabbing. You knew we would come get you."
- *Passion of the Christ:* "This isn't anti-Semitic. I'll tell you what is: those new *Star Wars* movies. Natalie Portman is a nice Jewish girl and a good actress, and what do they do? Give her a haircut that would startle a drag queen and a script written by a dyslexic gorilla."

Objective #100: "Fix" a Newly Minted Theatre Person

We joke about cults a lot in this book, but if you really want to see a closed society with bizarre mores and practices, look no further than the theatre department of your local junior college. You tried to warn your friend Barbara about this when she signed up for a night class in "Acting and Stage Movement," but alas, she laughed it off. Now, a little more than halfway through the semester, she's started pronouncing her name "Bar-*bar*-a" and referring to anything she doesn't like as "*dreadfully* provincial, dahling." To her credit, she did get an audition for a local commercial, but she tanked it by showing up in "movement clothes" and insisting they hear her prepared monologue from *Long Day's Journey into Night* instead of the line, "I'm so crazy about *Montgomery* Ward, they put me in a *mental* ward!" Ordinarily you'd just wait it out, as you did with her four-week-long conversion to Sikhism, but Barbara is your ride to work, and she now likes to practice along to show tunes in the car. Before you have to sit through another one-woman production of *South Pacific*, snap her out of it.

Option 100.1: Superstition
CLASSICAL CONDITIONING

Theatre people have an enormous body of superstitions, all of which they take very seriously and naturally think are adorable. Every time Barbara interrupts your conversation to do her "mah, mah, mee, mo, moo" vocal exercises, say "Good luck, Macbeth!" and hand her a peacock feather. After you do this a few times, she'll fear she is too cursed ever to go near a theatre again.

Option 100.2: Her Big Break
ABUSE/TORTURE

Sometimes, the truth hurts. Announce, excitedly, that you've called in an old favor and gotten her an audition with an agent! This agent is, of course, a drunk you picked up at a local dive, hired for forty-five dollars, and quickly dressed up with a beret and a handful of cologne samples. Halfway through Barbara's first audition piece, a self-penned monologue in the style of Nora Ephron titled "God, the

Devil, and My Mother; or, How I Got This Way," the "agent" should turn his head to the side and vomit explosively (which is why you'll want to do this at her place). Once he finishes, he should turn to Barbara and say apologetically, "I'm sorry, that's just where you are as an actress. Have you thought about real estate?"

> ### QUOTABLE: A BRIEF EXCERPT FROM "GOD, THE DEVIL, AND MY MOTHER"
>
> ". . . later that day, after Mom had bought me some Kotex and I had calmed down, she took me to get ice cream. She tried to talk to me about how I was going through a transition, to tell me that I was becoming a woman. I watched as my ice cream melted, the maraschino cherry slid down the mound of whipped cream and left red tracks that reminded me of earlier. I thought that if this was what being a woman was, I wanted no part of it. Suddenly, Mother leaned forward and whispered urgently, 'And remember! Soon you'll have bosoms!' I could have died of embarrassment. So far, growing up sucked, and Judy Blume had a lot to answer for."

Objective #101: Get Your Wife to Stop Being Vegan

Your wife Jenny has thrown every nonvegan item of food out of the house, leaving you stocked with only paprika and an old sweet potato with a three-inch vine at one end. Every time you come home from work, she smells your breath for the telltale odor of animal or animal by-product. All of this comes under the umbrella of "for better or for worse"—just—but today you discovered Jenny's post on the popular vegan online forum "The VEGina Monologues" titled "Newbie organic locavore vegan married to unenlightened carnivore—help!" There were sixty-eight responses, including Eats_Shoots_n_Leaves's recommendation of a competent vegan divorce lawyer (the divorce decree is printed in cruelty-free ink) and RadicalVeg1848's "thought experiment" in which she concludes that it would be okay for your wife to kill you since in the long run it would save *thousands* of animals. All this, just because she fell asleep with the TV on right before a *Food, Inc./Super-Size Me/ Fast Food Nation* night-owl triple-header, and absorbed it all in her sleep. Change the menu with a few brainwashing techniques.

Option 101.1: Burger Time

`PROJECT MK-ULTRA`

You know how those former drug addicts who speak at high schools always say they became addicted on their first hit? No one really talks about it, but meat—delicious, mouth-watering meat—is much the same way. Lock your wife in the bedroom with a double bacon cheeseburger until you hear chewing and little contented moans. If she was normal before, it should only take one bite of the meat to snap her out of her veg trance, but have a steak on the grill just in case.

Option 101.2: The Hard Part Is Renting the Pig

`ABUSE/TORTURE`

Post-traumatic stress disorder gets a bad rap, but like most mental illnesses, it has its redeeming features. If your wife has a terrible experience with a commonly eaten animal, the rage may drive her to eat them again out of a thirst for revenge. Rent a pig from an open-minded farmer and stow it in your wife's bathroom. Circle around the outside of the house to the bathroom window, and start throwing pebbles at the pig to annoy it. When Jenny opens the door, ready to wash her face and prepare to greet the day, she will immediately be confronted by an angry, squalling hog, which will probably charge her. She will not be so pleasantly disposed to the common hog or any of its fellow "nonhuman animal beings" after that.

QUOTABLE: WHAT YOUR WIFE SAID AFTER SHE MANAGED TO FLUSH THE PIG INTO THE SIDE YARD AND CONFRONTED YOU

"Dammit, Claude! A three-hundred-pound hog in my bathroom, just so I would *change my diet?* Have you completely lost your sense of scale? Look at this. It ate all my eye shadow and . . . oh, *dammit*, Claude. Look at that hooked rug. My mother made that when—no, leave it. It's not worth saving. We'll have to carry it out on a tarp or it'll drip on the carpet. Couldn't you have just made bacon until my resolve weakened? Did we have to have *farm animals where I brush my teeth?* I can't look at you right now. Go out and get me a meatball sub and don't talk to me."

CONCLUSION

Good for you! You've managed to avoid the wrath of God and the local law enforcement long enough to make it through this book. By now you're an expert in controlling the minds of those around you in an array of situations. What's important to remember at this point is to use your newfound powers for good and not evil. Or at least neutral. Idi Amin started out innocently enough by trying to score a few extra cherries in his Shirley Temple at the local T.G.I. Friday's, but the power went to his head and seven years later he was eating people and hiding out in Libya. Not to get all "Uncle Ben" with you, but clearly with great power comes great responsibility. Other people's minds may be your toys, but they're *expensive* toys. So don't just break them like a Malibu Barbie, *treasure* them like a special-edition 50th anniversary NASCAR Barbie. Now, go play.

ABOUT THE AUTHORS

Meghan Rowland and Chris Turner-Neal, formerly Magda Olynoff and Heinrich von Pfalz-von Kessen, are authors of *The Misanthrope's Guide to Life*. They also write the award-winning comedy blog, *www.2birds1blog.com*, a collection of crass musings, investigative reporting, and sarcasm; widely hailed as "the Thinking Man's *Beavis and Butthead*," the blog has been recognized by NPR, the *Washington Post*, and the Blogger's Choice Awards. When not writing, Meghan and Chris enjoy democracy, baseball, mom's apple pie, and reporting the names of their former comrades to the proper authorities. They've never been so happy.

Meghan lives in Washington, DC, and Chris lives in Philadelphia, PA.